THE UNKNOWN GOD

THE UNKNOWN GOD

Agnostic Essays

ANTHONY KENNY

continuum
LONDON • NEW YORK

CONTINUUM

The Tower Building
11 York Road
London SE1 7NX

15 East 26th Street
New York
NY 10010

www.continuumbooks.com

First published 2004
Reprinted 2004
This edition published 2005

British Library Cataloguing-in-Publication Data
A catalogue record for this book is available from the British Library.

ISBN 0–8264–7634–1

Typeset by RefineCatch Ltd, Bungay, Suffolk
Printed and bound by MPG Books Ltd, Bodmin, Cornwall

Contents

CONTENTS

Introduction

This book is a collection of essays written during the last fifteen years on topics related to the philosophy of religion. I have been reflecting and writing on these topics for more than 50 years now. In 1952, as a philosophy student at the Pontifical Gregorian University in Rome, I submitted a dissertation on a book by the Oxford theologian Austin Farrer, *Finite and Infinite*.[1] That book provided a rich and stylish introduction to the discipline of natural theology. Six years later, by now in priest's orders, I wrote a dissertation for a doctorate in theology at the Gregorian on 'The Philosophy of Linguistic Analysis and the Language of Religion'.

Though my thesis was accepted, and I passed all the necessary examinations, I did not proceed to take my doctorate at the Gregorian. There were two reasons for this. One was that it was a requirement that the dissertation be published, and I did not regard it as publishable. The other was that to take the degree one

---

[1] Austin Farrer, *Finite and Infinite* (London: Dacre Press, 1943).

had to subscribe to an anti-modernist oath, which included the statement that it was possible to prove the existence of God. This I had come to doubt. God's existence could be known, perhaps; but by way of proof?

By 1963 I had become too doubtful of several of the teachings of the Catholic Church to continue as a priest, and I returned to the life of a layman, becoming in 1964 a fellow of Balliol College and tutor in philosophy there. I continued to ponder the question whether it was possible to prove God's existence. The best place for an enquiry, I thought, would be the Five Ways of St Thomas Aquinas, the best-known and most revered of the proofs on offer. On careful examination I was unable to find that any of the arguments were successful; they depended more than met the eye on a background of outdated Aristotelian cosmology, and in places contained identifiable fallacies of argument. I published these negative results in a book *The Five Ways*.[2]

I turned next to a consideration of the divine nature. What were the attributes that believers assigned to divinity, and were they all compatible with each other? While holding the Wilde Lecturership in Natural Religion in Oxford, I gave three courses: one on omniscience, one on omnipotence and one on benevolence. I argued that there was an incompatibility between these attributes as standardly conceived, an incompatibility which could be brought out by reflection on the

[2] Anthony Kenny, *The Five Ways* (London: Routledge & Kegan Paul, 1969).

relationship between divine power and human freedom. If God is to have infallible knowledge of future human actions, then determinism must be true. If God is to escape responsibility for human wickedness, then determinism must be false. Hence, in the notion of a God who foresees all sins but is the author of none there lurks a contradiction: there cannot be an immutable, omniscient, omnipotent, all-good being. I presented the case in a book-length version of the lectures, *The God of the Philosophers*.[3]

There is no such thing, I concluded, as the God of scholastic or rationalist philosophy; but of course that is not the only possible conception of God, and I left open the question of the conceivability, and credibility, of a God described in less absolute terms. I have remained agnostic on this issue from that time to the present, but subsequent reflection has made me ever more doubtful of the possibility of applying to anything whatever, in a literal sense, the predicates which have traditionally been used to construct the concept of Godhead. At the same time, I have become more interested in the possibility of interpreting religious discourse in a poetic rather than a scientific mode.

The present collection of essays reflects this strand of thought. The essays fall into six groups which make up a coherent pattern of argument and reflection.

The first essay, 'The Ineffable Godhead', stands on its own. It sums up the theme of the book: that both

---

[3] Anthony Kenny, *The God of the Philosophers* (Oxford: Oxford University Press, 1978).

theological tradition and philosophical analysis lead one to conclude that the possibility of literal description of God is extremely limited, and encourage one to explore the possibility of understanding religious language metaphorically.

The next two essays form a pair. They illustrate the book's general theme while starting out from a theological standpoint, namely the account of God given in St Anselm's *Proslogion*. The first essay of the pair, 'Anselm on the Conceivability of God' describes how St Anselm's premises lead to the conclusion that nothing can be literally said about God. The second essay ('Metaphor, Analogy and Agnosticism') explores the possibility of taking descriptions of God as true in something other than a literal sense.

The next group of essays approaches the same topic starting out from a philosophical basis. The first of the pair 'God and Mind' analyses the mentalistic predicates which we apply to human beings. The second, 'The Limits of Anthropomorphism', shows the extreme difficulty of applying such predicates meaningfully to a being with the traditional attributes of divinity.

The sixth and seventh essays take these themes further. 'The Problem of Evil and the Argument from Design' shows that there are problems not just with describing God as a person, but also with applying to him evaluative predicates. 'Faith, Pride and Humility' defends the agnostic stance here adopted from the charge of arrogance: on the contrary, I argue, agnosticism is a more humble attitude than either faith or atheism.

From this point on the book turns from the exposition of my own theses to the presentation of other writers' positions. Anyone who believes, as I do, that religious language has an irreducibly metaphorical element must take seriously the expression of religion by poets; and the eighth essay compares with each other the writings of two Victorian agnostic poets, Arthur Hugh Clough and Matthew Arnold. The Victorian theme is followed up in the ninth and tenth essays, which discuss John Henry Newman, the most articulate of nineteenth-century believers in England, and Leslie Stephen, the most eloquent champion of agnosticism.

The sixth and final section of the book deals with the work of the twentieth-century philosopher, Ludwig Wittgenstein. His thought is relevant to the topics of the earlier essays for two reasons. First of all, the analysis of mind and the critique of anthropomorphism in the fourth and fifth essays depend heavily on Wittgenstein's teaching; but it is important to separate the elements in his thought which lead to the agnostic position from the crude atheism of the logical positivists, who tried to rule out religious language as meaningless on the basis of some principle of verification. This I try to do in the eleventh essay. Second, Wittgenstein's own philosophy of religion, though never presented systematically, has seemed to many to offer a further choice over and above theism, agnosticism and atheism. Personally, I am doubtful of this claim, but none the less I find some of Wittgenstein's *obiter dicta* on religious topics illuminating and exciting, and for this reason I have included them in the twelfth and final essay.

Six of these essays have appeared in print before; six of them have never been published. The first began life as a Warburton lecture at Lincoln's Inn, and was published by that Honourable Society in the series of Warburton Lectures for 1985–1994. The second and third, lectures delivered to symposia in Rome in 1989 and 1991 respectively, were published in *Archivio di Filosofia*.[4] The fourth and fifth have not previously been published; they are revisions of Stanton Lectures given in Cambridge in the 1980s. The sixth, again a paper presented to a Rome symposium, was published in *Archivio di Filosofia*.[5] The seventh was originally a university sermon preached in Oxford.[6] Essay 8 has not been published. Essay 9 appeared first in *Newman, a Man for our Time*.[7] Essay 10, a Leslie Stephen Lecture delivered in Cambridge, has never been published. Essay 11 was published in *Wittgenstein: Mind and Language*.[8] Essay 12 has never been published. Essays 2, 6 and 9 appeared in *What is Faith?*[9]

Anthony Kenny, 1 August 2003

[4] *Archivio di Filosofia* (Padua: 1989, 1991), LVIII, LX.

[5] Ibid. (1988), LVI.

[6] A paper derived from it was published in *Bene Scripsisti*, the *Festschrift* for Stanislav Sousedik (Prague 2002).

[7] David Brown (ed.), *Newman, a Man for our Time* (London: SPCK 1990).

[8] R. Egidi (ed.), *Wittgenstein: Mind and Language* (Rome: Kluwer, 1995).

[9] Anthony Kenny, *What is Faith* (Oxford: Oxford University Press, 1992).

1

The Ineffable Godhead

It is notoriously difficult to determine the will of God in respect of human social and political issues. Alexander Pope, in the fourth Epistle of his *Essay on Man* illustrates the way in which the fortunes and misfortunes of God's cosmos fall on virtue and vice alike. Then he continues:

> But still this world (so fitted for the knave)
> Contents us not. A better shall we have?
> A kingdom of the Just then let it be:
> But first consider how those Just agree.
> The good must merit God's peculiar care;
> But who, but God, can tell us who they are?
> One thinks on Calvin heaven's own spirit fell,
> Another deems him instrument of hell;
> If Calvin feel Heaven's blessing, or its rod,
> This cries there is, and that, there is no God.
> What shocks one part will edify the rest,
> Nor with one system can they all be blest.

In the twentieth century philosophers in the English-speaking world have been keen to emphasize not only the difficulty of stating God's will on particular issues, but the difficulty for human beings of saying anything intelligible at all about the nature of God. It is probably not straining the truth to say that a substantial majority of philosophers in this country in the last 50 years have been atheists of one kind or another.

This may, perhaps, be a rash statement. If a pollster approaches a philosopher with the question 'Do you believe in God?' the answer may very well be 'Well, it depends on what you mean by "God".' But even if questioner and answerer agree on a meaning – e.g. all-knowing, all-powerful, all-good being who created the universe – there may still be reluctance to give a yes/no answer.

One reason for the philosopher's reluctance may be that there is an ambiguity in saying 'I do not believe there is a God.' Someone who says such a thing may mean 'I believe there is no God': the speaker is a positive atheist, someone who positively believes in the non-existence of God. Or what is meant may be something less definite: 'I have no belief that there is a God': such a person is only a negative atheist, someone who lacks a belief in the existence of God. A negative atheist is an a-theist or non-theist in the sense of not being a theist or believer in the existence of God. But the negative atheist is not necessarily a positive atheist: she may lack not only a belief in the existence of God but also a belief in the non-existence of God. If the question had been 'Is there a God?' she would not have answered 'yes' and she would not have answered 'no'; she would have answered 'I don't know'.

Within negative atheism there is a further crucial distinction to be made. Those who lack the belief in God may do so either because they think that the statement 'God exists' is meaningful but uncertain, or because they think that the sentence is not really meaningful at all. Thus, one of the most celebrated nineteenth-century atheists, Charles Bradlaugh, expressed his own atheism thus: 'The Atheist does not say "There is no God", but he says "I know not what you mean by God; I am without the idea of God; the word 'God' is to me a sound conveying no clear or distinct affirmation." '

The belief that religious language is meaningless was to have considerable popularity among philosophers in the first half of the twentieth century and up to the present day.

Those who fail to believe in God because they think that the truth-value of 'God exists' is uncertain may be called agnostic negative atheists, or agnostics for short. They are people who do not know whether there is a God but think that there is, in this area, a truth to be known. Those who think that religious language is meaningless think that the sentence 'God exists' does not have any truth-value, even an unknown truth-value; they think there is no truth to be known here at all. To refer to this class of negative atheists we might use the (superficially paradoxical) expression 'positivist negative atheists', or, more concisely 'positivists'.

The name is appropriate because the most systematic endeavour to show that religious language was meaningless was made by the logical positivist philosophers in the 1930s and by their successors after the Second

World War. The thesis that talk about God is in an important sense meaningless had as one of its best-known defenders Sir Alfred Ayer.

We should note that there is no room for dividing positive atheists into two classes in the way we have divided negative atheists. Someone who believes there is no God cannot say that religious language is meaningless: for if it is meaningless, his own utterance 'There is no God' is meaningless also. If 'God exists' lacks a truth-value, so does its negation.

There are, then, four positions which philosophers may adopt with respect to the proposition 'There is a God', as follows:

1. It is meaningless and neither true nor false: positivism.
2. It is meaningful and false: (positive) atheism.
3. It is meaningful and may be true or false: agnosticism.
4. It is meaningful and true: theism.

The positivists based their position on the verifiability criterion of meaning: a statement has factual meaning, they claimed, if and only if it is empirically verifiable. But statements about God are not verifiable even in principle, they argued, and therefore they lack factual meaning.

Some theists have tried to defend the meaningfulness of religious language by saying that statements about God are in principle capable of empirical verification: they have appealed to religious experience in support of the existence of God. Many more have rejected the verifiability principle itself as being extremely implausible even outside the religious context. In my view, this is correct; but here I want to bring out the difficulty of speaking coherently about God not from the hostile position of the positivists but from the traditional doctrine of the ineffability of God. The doctrine that, in some sense, it is quite impossible to speak about God; that God is not something to be captured by human language.

Theistic philosophers, through the ages, have sought to show that there is a God by offering proofs of his existence. This procedure itself, I would claim, brings out the difficulty in making meaningful statements about God. Proofs of the existence of God are classified by philosophers into two main kinds. There are ontological proofs, which start from the concept of God and show that the very existence of the idea of God shows that there must be a God in reality. The most famous ontological proof is the proof of St Anselm, the eleventh-century archbishop of Canterbury. There are cosmological proofs, which start from a phenomenon, or class of phenomena, within the world. These phenomena, such proofs insist, demand explanation. They go on to show that a particular type of explanation will not lead to intellectual satisfaction, however frequently it is applied. Thus movement is not to be explained by objects in motion, nor can effects be explained ultimately by causes which are themselves in turn effects, nor can complexity be explained by beings which are themselves complex.

The most famous cosmological proofs are the Five Ways of the thirteenth-century theologian, St Thomas Aquinas.

It is a mistake to think that a cosmological argument seeks to show that God is the terminus of any of the normal patterns of explanation in the world. Rather, the concept of God is invoked as a limiting case of explanation. If a proof of the existence of God is to take its start from an explanatory series in the world, it must aim to show that such a series, however prolonged, cannot arrive at a complete and intellectually satisfactory account of the phenomena to be explained. The argument must take a form similar to the demonstration that the addition of one-half to one-quarter to one-eighth . . . and so on, will never exceed unity.

If we are to have a proof of the existence of God it will not suffice to say that we do not know whether some pattern of explanation in the world will succeed in explaining everything that needs explaining; we have to aim to show that it cannot possibly do so. And that is indeed what the traditional proofs of God attempted to do: to show, for instance, that no explanation by one or more moving objects will suffice to explain motion, that no explanation of one contingent object by another contingent object will suffice to explain contingency.

If there is to be a successful version of the cosmological argument, it must be an argument to show that a particular type of explanation must fail to render intelligible the class of phenomena to be explained, and

12

that intelligibility can only be found, if at all, in a being which stands outside the application of that particular paradigm of explanation. Such a being, the argument may conclude in the style of St Thomas, is what all men call God; but it is not to be taken for granted that we understand without further ado what the nature of that 'calling' may be.

Cosmological proofs of the existence of God, if they are not to be mere appeals to ignorance and incomprehension, must not depend on particular features of the world which are as yet unexplained. They must depend on the necessary limits of particular types of explanation. The cosmological argument must depend on necessary, not contingent, features of the kind of cosmos to be explained. Otherwise they will be vulnerable to defeat by the progress of science. In my view the Five Ways of Aquinas are unsuccessful forms of the cosmological argument precisely because they depend, more than at first meets the eye, on particular outdated theories of physical explanation.

It is possible to look at proofs such as Aquinas's Five Ways as providing not so much proofs as definitions of God. God is then that which accounts for what, in the motion series, is left unexplained by previous motors in the series. God is that which accounts for that which, in the causal series, is left unexplained by the individual members of the series. God is that which accounts for what is left unexplained in the series of contingent substances which arise from each other and turn into each other. God is that which accounts for what is left explained in the series of complex entities composed of simpler entities.

The way in which God accounts for the unexplained is not by figuring in some further explanation. When we invoke God we do not explain the world, or any series of phenomena in the world. The mode of intelligibility which is provided by the invocation of God is something of a quite different kind. In terms of a distinction fashionable in some philosophical quarters, the introduction of the concept of God provides not explanation but understanding.

Because God is not a part of any of the explanatory series which he is invoked to account for – he is first mover unmoved, he is first cause only by analogy – the vocabulary and predicates of the different explanatory series are not applicable to him in any literal sense.

The ontological argument, no less than the cosmological argument, is an argument pointing to a limit. However, now the limit is not the limit of explanation but the limit of conception itself. The premise of the ontological argument is that each of us, even the atheist, has the concept of God as that than which no greater can be conceived. From this premise, St Anselm offers to prove that God must exist in reality and not only in the mind. But it is not to be forgotten that he goes on to say that that than which no greater can be conceived cannot itself be conceived.

When we turn from the cosmological argument to the ontological one, the vocabulary at our disposal to describe God becomes even more constrained. The ontological argument, in contrast to the cosmological argument, concerns not explanation but conception. God, in Anselm's definition, becomes the outer limit of conception; because anything than which something greater can be conceived is not God. God is not the greatest conceivable object; he is himself greater than can be conceived, therefore beyond the bounds of conception, and therefore literally inconceivable.

But if God is inconceivable, does that not mean that the notion of God is self-contradictory, and God a nonsensical *Unding* which cannot exist? That would be so if conceivability were mere freedom from contradiction; but there are many reasons for thinking that non-contradictoriness is not identical with freedom from contradiction. A notion is conceivable only if it is free from contradiction: that much is sure; but Kant, Wittgenstein and the positivists have suggested other, more stringent, criteria of conceivability. The conditions laid down by these philosophers seem unsatisfactory for reasons unconnected with theism; but they are right to say that freedom from contradiction is only a necessary and not a sufficient condition of conceivability.

If God is inconceivable, is it not self-refuting to talk about him at all, even if only to state his inconceivability? The paradox here is one which is familiar in other areas of philosophy too. Bertrand Russell gave currency to Berry's paradox, which invites us to consider the expression 'the least natural number not nameable in fewer than 22 syllables'. This expression names in 21 syllables a natural number which by definition cannot be named in fewer than 22 syllables.

Clearly, to solve this paradox we have at least to distinguish between different ways of *naming*. And the solution to the paradox of God, if there is to be one, must be found by insisting that while we can speak of God, we cannot speak of him literally.

If this is so, there cannot be any *science* of theology. The God of scholastic and rationalistic philosophy is an *Unding*, full of contradiction. Even in talking about God we must not contradict ourselves. Once we find ourselves uttering contradictory propositions, we must draw ourselves up. We can perhaps seek to show that the contradiction is only apparent; we may trace back the steps that led to the contradictory conclusion, in the hope that minor modification to one of the steps will remove the clash. Or we may claim that the contradiction arises because metaphorical language has mistakenly been taken literally. The one thing we must not do is to accept contradiction cheerfully.

To say that we cannot speak literally of God is to say – to use the currently fashionable philosophical jargon – that the word 'God' does not belong in a language-game. Literal truth is truth within a language-game. Some philosophers believe that there is a special religious language-game, and it is in that game that the concept of God is located. I believe, on the contrary, that there is no religious language-game, and that we speak of God in metaphor. And to use metaphor is to use a word in a language-game which is not its home.

However, it is not peculiar to theology that it cannot be encapsulated in a language-game. If Wittgenstein is right – and after all the notion of language-game is his coinage – there is no philosophical language-game either: there are no truths special to philosophy. Finally, a certain kind of poetry is an attempt to express what is literally inexpressible.

Metaphor, as has been said, is not a move in a language-game. It is, in the standard case, taking a word which has a role in one language-game and moving it to another. The predicates which we apply to God – predicates, for instance, concerning knowledge and love – are taken from other language-games, and used in the absence of the criteria which give them their meanings in the language-games in which they have their home. If there is such a thing as a religious language-game, it is not a language-game in which there is literal truth. In this, as was observed, religious language resembles philosophy and the kind of poetry which endeavours to express the literally inexpressible.

Not all poetry, of course, is of that kind. To recall again Pope – it would be foolish to say that

> Great Anna, whom three realms obey
> Did sometimes council take, and sometimes tea

is an attempt to express the inexpressible. It would also be foolish to claim that the poetry of the inexpressible is bound to be of superior value to the poetry of the mundane. But in order to throw light on the problems of talking about God, it is the poetry of the inexpressible to which we must turn.

I know of no philosopher who has described the paradox of talking about the inconceivable Godhead with such precision as the poet Arthur Hugh Clough.

Consider, as an example, his poem of 1851, 'ὕμνος ἄυμνος' ('A hymn, yet not a hymn'). Its first stanza begins with an invocation to the incomprehensible Godhead.

> O Thou whose image in the shrine
> Of human spirits dwells divine;
> Which from that precinct once conveyed,
> To be to outer day displayed,
> Doth vanish, part, and leave behind
> Mere blank and void of empty mind,
> Which wilful fancy seeks in vain
> With casual shapes to fill again.

The poem starts from the assumption that the place to look for God is in the individual's inmost soul. Attempts to give public expression to the God encountered in the soul yield only meaningless, self-contradictory utterances ('blank and void') or images unconnected with reality ('casual shapes').

The second stanza of the poem, which I omit, develops the theme of the impotence of human utterance to embody the divine. In the third, the poet proclaims that silence – inner as well as outer – is the only response to the ineffable:

> O thou, in that mysterious shrine
> Enthroned, as we must say, divine!
> I will not frame one thought of what
> Thou mayest either be or not.
> I will not prate of 'thus' and 'so'
> And be profane with 'yes' and 'no'.
> Enough that in our soul and heart
> Thou, whatso'er thou may'st be, art.

The agnosticism is radical: the *via negativa* is rejected as firmly as the *via positiva*. Not only can we not say of God what he is, we are equally impotent to say what he is not. The possibility, therefore, cannot be ruled out that one or other of the revelations claimed by others may after all be true:

> Unseen, secure in that high shrine
> Acknowledged present and divine
> I will not ask some upper air,
> Some future day, to place thee there;
> Nor say, nor yet deny, Such men
> Or women saw thee thus and then:
> Thy name was such, and there or here
> To him or her thou didst appear.

In the final stanza Clough pushes his agnosticism a stage further. Perhaps there is no way in which God dwells – even ineffably – as an object of the inner vision of the soul. Perhaps we should reconcile ourselves to the idea that God is not to be found at all by human minds. But even that does not take off all possibility of prayer.

> Do only thou in that dim shrine,
> Unknown or known, remain, divine;
> There, or if not, at least in eyes
> That scan the fact that round them lies.
> The hand to sway, the judgement guide,
> In sight and sense, thyself divide:
> Be thou but there – in soul and heart,
> I will not ask to feel thou art.

The soul reconciled to the truth that there can be no

analogue of seeing or feeling God, that nothing can be meaningfully said about him, can yet address him and pray to be illuminated by his power and be the instrument of his action. But does not this presume that God can after all be described: at least as a powerful agent who can hear our prayers? No, the prayer need not assume the truth of that; only its *possibility* is needed. An agnostic's praying to a God whose existence he doubts is no more unreasonable than the act of a man adrift in the ocean, or stranded on a mountainside, who cries for help though he may never be heard, or fires a signal which may never be seen. Of course the need for help need not be the only motive which may drive an agnostic to prayer: the desire to give thanks for the beauty and wonder of the world may be another.

If there is a religious language-game, it is surely the language-game of worship. This, too, has received magisterial description in a poem of Clough's: his early work, 'Qui Laborat, Orat':

> O only Source of all our light and life,
> Whom as our truth, our strength, we see and feel
> But whom the hours of mortal moral strife
> Alone aright reveal!
>
> Mine inmost soul, before Thee inly brought,
> Thy presence owns ineffable, divine;
> Chastised each rebel self-encentred thought,
> My will adoreth Thine.
>
> With eye down-dropt, if then this earthly mind
> Speechless remain, or speechless e'en depart;

Nor seek to see – for what of earthly kind
Can see Thee as Thou art?

If well-assured, 'tis but profanely bold
In thought's abstractest forms to seem to see,
It dare not dare thee dread communion hold
In ways unworthy Thee.

O not unowned, Thou shalt unnamed forgive,
In worldly walks the prayerless heart prepare;
And if in work its life it seem to live,
Shalt make that work be prayer.

Nor times shall lack, when while the work it plies
Unsummoned powers the blinding film shall part
And scarce by happy tears made, the eyes
In recognition start.

But, as thou willest, give or e'en forbear
The beatific supersensual sight,
So, with Thy blessing blest, that humbler prayer
Approach Thee morn and night.

The poem has appealed to many readers – Tennyson
was among its first admirers. It has been applauded by
the devout no less than the sceptic, and it has subtleties
which are worth attention. There is first the paradox,
obvious and surely intentional, that a poem which
appears to deny the propriety of addressing the
Godhead in prayer is itself an explicit second-person
address to God. What is the inward bringing of the
inmost soul before God but that 'lifting up of the mind
and heart to God' which is one of the traditional

definitions of prayer? The poet, therefore, is not so much attacking the practice of vocal prayer as urging the praying soul to be aware of the limitations of human prayer, even at the moment of uttering one.

The first two stanzas, in particular, in their majestic movement, could stand by themselves as a prayer that might be uttered without misgiving by a perfectly orthodox Christian. They would, no doubt, be most congenial to those traditions which have emphasized the inner light rather than the external revelation as the supreme source of our awareness of God. But the solemn *rallentando* forced by the alliteration of the last two lines of the first stanza makes the beginning of the poem remarkably apt for liturgical recitation.

The second pair of stanzas develop, now in a more radical fashion, the traditional themes of the spirituality and ineffability of God. Because God is spirit, he cannot be seen by human eye, nor pictured by any inner eye of the imagination. Because God is ineffable, his nature cannot be expressed in language, and therefore it cannot be grasped by any human thought however abstract. Thus far many theologians of the most orthodox kind would agree with the sentiment of the poem. But must the conclusion be that the inner eye must be cast down and the inner voice be silenced?

The ineffability of God is given by Clough a moral as well as a logical element. Man must not attempt to name God, as Adam named the animals; for naming is a claiming of power. When God named himself to Moses it was in a manner which was a refusal to give a name. To leave God unnamed, then, is not equivalent to disowning him; on the contrary it is to refuse to claim an ownership which would be blasphemous.

Another moral consideration enters into the contention that it is impossible to talk literally about God. (This too is developed by Clough, in some of his prose writings.) The fact that theological language cannot be literal provides a reason for toleration in religion. That is to say, theological propositions cannot contradict each other in the straightforward way in which empirical propositions do. Hence, there is not that head-on clash between different theologies, and different religions, which has been used to justify the persecution and killing of one religious group by others.

To say that religious language is not literal, and to say that different religious creeds do not contradict each other, is not to say that all religions are of equal worth. The mode of utterance of Shakespeare and of William McGonagall is poetic in each case; that does not mean that the writings of each of them display an equal insight into human nature. Equally, the fact that Christianity and Hinduism each speak in metaphor does not necessitate that each of them has an equally valuable insight into divine nature, or the nature of the universe as a whole.

The premises of Clough's 'Qui Laborat, Orat' are profoundly orthodox; the guiding sentiment too is traditional. *Orando laborando* was Rugby's school motto; but a closer parallel to the poem's title is the motto of the Benedictine order: *Laborare est orare*. But from the ineffability of God orthodox believers have never drawn the conclusion that it is profane to use words to describe and invoke him. Rather, they have said, with Saint Augustine, *vae tacentibus de te* – woe to those who are silent about thee.

Some religious thinkers have attempted to show that coherent literal description of God is after all possible; others have simply claimed that there can be worse things than talking nonsense. Perhaps that is what lies behind Augustine's *vae tacentibus*. We may aim at a rational worship, and yet get no further than the babble of infants or the glossolaly of the possessed.

In the twentieth century no man surpassed Wittgenstein in the devotion of sharp intelligence to the demarcation of the boundary between sense and nonsense. Wittgenstein finished the masterpiece of his youth with the words 'Wovon man nicht sprechen kann, darüber muss man schweigen': whereof one cannot speak, thereof one must be silent. But within ten years he was putting forth his own gloss on Augustine's *vae tacentibus*: 'Was, du Mistviech, du willst keinen Unsinn reden? Rede nur einen Unsinn, es macht nichts.'[1] Which we may paraphrase thus: 'So you don't want to talk nonsense, do you, you cowpat? Go on, talk nonsense; it won't do you any harm.'

---

[1] F. Waismann and B.F. McGuinness, *Ludwig Wittgenstein und der Wiener Kreis* (Oxford: Blackwell, 1967), p. 69.

2

Anselm on the Conceivability of God

Is the ontological argument valid? Professor Timothy Smiley of Cambridge once offered a succinct and trenchant argument in favour of its validity. Define the ontological argument, he said, as the best possible argument for the existence of God. Now clearly an argument for the existence of God which is valid is better than an argument for his existence which is invalid. Therefore the best possible argument for the existence of God is valid, and so the ontological argument is valid.

I shall not in this essay be concerned with the validity of the ontological argument: I doubt if I can offer, in brief compass, anything which would improve on Professor Smiley's entertaining presentation. Instead, I shall discuss what would follow about the conceivability of God if we were to follow the line of thought of Anselm in the *Proslogion*.

Let us begin by making a contrast between the

ontological argument and other forms of argument to the existence of God, such as the different versions of the cosmological argument. All such proofs start from a phenomenon, or class of phenomena, within the world, which demand explanation. They go on to show that a particular type of explanation will not lead to intellectual satisfaction, however frequently it is applied. Thus movement is not to be explained by objects in motion, nor can effects be explained ultimately by causes which are themselves in turn effects, nor can complexity be explained by beings which are themselves complex.

Proofs of the existence of God, if they are not to be mere appeals to ignorance and incomprehension, must not depend on particular features of the world which are yet unexplained.

The appeal to God is not based on particular failures of explanation but upon the provable inability of a particular pattern of explanation to give an intellectually satisfying understanding of phenomena of a certain type.

Consider, for instance, the relationship of the argument from design to Darwinian explanation by evolution. The theist position and the evolutionary one are not competing explanations of the same fact. However successful explanation by natural selection may be in explaining the origin of particular species of life, it clearly cannot explain how there come to be such things as species at all. That is to say, it cannot explain how there came to be true breeding populations; since the existence of such populations is one of the premises on which explanations in terms of natural selection rest as their starting-point.

To say this is not to say that Darwinians do not offer explanations of the origin of life; of course they do, but they are explanations of a radically different kind from explanation by natural selection. Whether God must be invoked as the author of life, or whether one of the explanations of life in terms of chance and necessity can be made intellectually satisfactory, one thing is clear: natural selection cannot explain the origin of species.

The nature of theistic argument here is often mis-understood by exponents of evolution. One can illustrate this by referring to the work of Richard Dawkins, whose book *The Blind Watchmaker* is one of the most lucid expositions of natural selection in the English language. Dawkins considers the following argument offered to show the difficulties of accounting for the origin of life and the existence of the original machinery of replication:

> Cumulative selection can manufacture complexity while single-step selection cannot. But cumulative selection can-not work unless there is some minimal machinery of repli-cation and replicator power, and the only machinery of replication that we know seems too complicated to have come into existence by means of anything less than many generations of cumulative selection.[1]

This argument, Dawkins says, is sometimes offered

---

[1] Richard Dawkins, *The Blind Watchmaker* (Harlow: Longman, 1986), p. 141.

as proof of an intelligent designer, the creator of DNA and protein. He replies:

> This is a transparently feeble argument, indeed it is obviously self-defeating. Organized complexity is the thing we are having difficulty in explaining. Once we are allowed simply to postulate organized complexity if only the organized complexity of the DNA/protein-replicating engine, it is relatively easy to invoke it as a generator of yet more organized complexity. That, indeed, is what most of this book is about. But of course any God capable of intelligently designing something as complex as the DNA/protein-replicating machine must have been at least as complex and organized as that machine itself. Far more so if we suppose him *additionally* capable of such advanced functions as listening to prayers and forgiving sins. To explain the origin of the DNA/protein machine by invoking a supernatural Designer is to explain precisely nothing, for it leaves unexplained the origin of the Designer. You have to say something like 'God was always there' and if you allow yourself that kind of lazy way out, you might as well just say 'DNA; was always there' or 'Life was always there', and be done with it.[2]

A traditional theist would say that this paragraph misrepresented the notion of God in two ways. First of all, God is as much outside the series complexity/simplicity as he is outside the series mover/moved. He is not complex as a protein is; nor, for that matter, is he simple as an elementary particle is. He has neither the simplicity nor the complexity of material objects.

[2] Ibid.

Secondly, he is not one of a series of temporal contingents, each requiring explanation in terms of a previous state of the universe: unchanging and everlasting, he is outside the temporal series.

Because God is not a part of any of the explanatory series which he is invoked to account for – he is an unmoved mover, he, is first cause only by analogy – the vocabulary and predicates of the different explanatory series are not applicable to him in any literal sense.

But when we turn from the cosmological argument to the ontological one, the vocabulary at our disposal to describe God becomes even more constrained. The ontological argument, in contrast to the cosmological argument, concerns not explanation but conception. God, in Anselm's definition, becomes the outer limit of conception; because anything than which something greater can be conceived is not God. God is not the greatest conceivable object (and this is one reason why Professor Smiley's version of the ontological argument is only a joke). God is himself greater than can be conceived, therefore beyond the bounds of conception, and therefore literally inconceivable.

If God is inconceivable, is it not self-refuting to talk about him at all, even if only to state his inconceivability? Let us look more closely at Anselm's text to see how he handles this difficulty.

The fool says in his heart there is no God; that is to say he thinks (*cogitat*) that there is no God. On the other hand, he hears, and understands (*intelligit*) *that than which no greater can be thought*. So he thinks that that than which no greater can be thought does not exist. But how can this be since that than which no greater can be thought cannot be thought not to exist?[3] This is the question which is posed by Chapter 4: if saying in the heart is thinking, how could the fool say in his heart what cannot be thought?

Anselm appears to reply by making a distinction between two senses of 'thought' (*non uno modo cogitatur*). In one sense, I think of something if I think of a word which signifies it; in another sense I think of a thing only if I understand that which the thing is in itself. The fool can understand the words 'that than which nothing greater can be thought'; he can only deny the existence of God because he does not understand the reality which lies behind the words.

The solution to the paradox which faces Anselm cannot be solved simply by distinguishing between two different ways of *thinking*. For Anselm goes on to say that not only the fool but none of us understands what lies behind the words 'that than which nothing greater can be thought'. Let us consider a number of passages which leave the matter beyond doubt.

God lives in inaccessible light: his goodness is incomprehensible. His goodness is beyond all understanding (*bonitas quae sic omnem intellectum excedis*).[4] The soul strains to see but it cannot see anything beyond what it sees except darkness – but it does not really see darkness, for there is no darkness in God, but

---

[3] Anselm, *Proslogion*, Chapter 3.
[4] Ibid., Chapter 9.

it sees that it cannot see further because of its own darkness.[5] God is not only that than which no greater can be thought but is himself something greater than can be thought (*Non solum es quo maius cogitari nequit, sed es quiddam maius quam cogitari possit*).[6]

There is nothing self-contradictory in saying that that than which no greater can be thought is itself too great for thought: 'that than which no greater can be thought' is not equivalent to 'the greatest possible object of thought'. I can say that my copy of the *Proslogion* is something than which nothing larger will fit into my pocket. That is true, but it does not mean that my copy of the *Proslogion* will itself fit into my pocket: in fact it is far too big to do so.

But we may ask what sort of *cogitatio* Anselm has in mind here: the sort that deals with the words for things or the sort that deals with the essence of things? The distinction made earlier will not help here. For if God is literally ineffable, then there are not words to denote and describe him as there are words to describe and denote other things.

In the reply to Gaunilo Anselm makes no systematic distinction between being thought of and being understood: what is in the intellect and what is thought of appear to be the same. The distinction drawn there is rather between being in the intellect and being fully understood: 'Perhaps you say that something which is

---

[5] Ibid., Chapter 14.
[6] Ibid., Chapter 15.

not fully understood is not understood at all and is not in the intellect. If so, you will have to tell me that someone who cannot look at the direct light of the sun does not see the daylight, which is nothing but the light of the sun.'[7]

We cannot look at the sun, but we see the sun's light: we are invited to draw the parallel in the case of God.

Later in the reply a distinction is drawn between *intelligere* and *cogitare*, but on a basis different from the distinction between two sorts of thought that is drawn in the *Proslogion*. Now the distinction seems to be on the basis that one can understand (*intelligere*) only what is true, but one can think (*cogitare*) also what is false. 'Nothing of what is can be understood not to be, but everything – except the one being – can be thought not to be.'[8]

Anselm's last word on the topic of the ineffability of God comes in the ninth chapter of the reply to Gaunilo:

Even if it were true that that than which no greater can be thought cannot itself be thought or understood, it would not follow that it would be false that 'that than which no greater can be thought' could be thought and understood. Nothing prevents something being called ineffable, even though that which is called ineffable cannot itself be said; and likewise the unthinkable can be thought, even though what is rightly called unthinkable cannot be thought. So, when 'that than which no greater can be thought' is spoken

[7] Ibid., Chapter 2.
[8] Ibid.

of, there is no doubt that what is heard can be thought and understood, even though the thing itself, than which no greater can be thought, cannot be thought or understood.

Subtle as it is, this paragraph does not really solve the problem. How is it possible to know what a word means if what it means cannot even be thought about? If a thing is ineffable, what is one saying when one tries to identify the thing? The distinction between understanding words and understanding the thing which they describe can only be effective if the things in question are to some *extent* describable.

Anselm's problem, in his own terms, seems insoluble. Does the difficulty apply to all attempts to talk about God? Not *necessarily*. A possible solution may be found by making a distinction between two kinds of ineffability: by exploring the suggestion that while we can speak of God, we cannot speak of him literally. God, if that is so, will be literally ineffable, but metaphorically describable. This suggestion I will explore further in the next essay.

3

Metaphor, Analogy and Agnosticism

In the previous essay I expounded the difficulty which faced St Anselm in talking about a God who was not just something than which nothing greater can be thought but something that was itself greater than could be thought. How can he avoid the conclusion that the word 'God' is meaningless? How is it possible to know what a word means if what it means cannot even be thought about? If a thing is ineffable, what is one saying when one tries to identify the thing? Anselm attempts to make a distinction *between* understanding words and understanding the thing which they describe. But this distinction can only be effective if the things in question are to some extent describable and to that extent are not ineffable, as Anselm believed that God was.

Anselm's problem, in his own terms, seems insoluble. At the end of the previous essay I suggested that a solution might be found by making a distinction between two kinds of ineffability: by exploring the suggestion that while we can speak of God, we cannot speak of him literally. God, if that is so, will be literally ineffable, but metaphorically describable.

To say that we cannot speak literally of God is to say that the word 'God' does not belong in a language-game. Literal truth is truth within a language-game. I have argued that there is no religious language-game, and that we speak of God in metaphor. And to use metaphor is to use a word in a language-game that is not its home.

Some conceptions of God are self-cancelling or self-contradictory; not in the patent way in which 'square circle' is self-cancelling, but in the less accessible way in which 'omniscient omnipotent being who is not responsible for human wickedness' – I have argued elsewhere – involves self-contradiction. Note that self-cancelling phrases are not nonsensical or meaningless. On the contrary, it is precisely because we do see the meaning of 'square circle' that we know that it cannot function as a name. It is because we know the sense of the expression 'square circle' that we know that it cannot have a reference. I would also want to argue that it is because we can tease out the sense of certain traditional philosophical definitions of Godhead that we know that the word 'God', so understood, cannot have a reference. There is a distinction between self-contradiction (patent or latent) and meaninglessness.

There are two kinds of meaninglessness. There is the meaninglessness of something that has had no meaning assigned to it: as in the case of the nonsense sounds which philosophers produce as examples of nonsense words, or the ill-formed strings of words which they produce as examples of nonsense sentences. But there is the meaninglessness which results not from the lack of any attempt to assign a meaning, but, rather from the failure of a bona fide attempt. If God-talk is meaningless, it is clearly in the second sense.

What is the difference between an atheist's saying that the existence of the universe is a mystery to which we do not know the answer, and a theist's saying that the answer to the question about the existence of the universe is a God about whom we cannot know anything? In this essay I want to pursue the answer to this question. Some philosophers, such as Kant, would reject the idea that the existence of the universe is a mystery to which we do not know the answer. For Kant, statements about the universe as a whole are illegitimate; hence questions about the universe as a whole are, for him, ill-formed questions, not questions whose answer is unknown. I am unconvinced by the arguments which lead to this conclusion.

I have no systematic objection to talk of 'the cause of world as a whole'. Indeed, we can make some true statements which are – at least prima facie – about the cause of the world as a whole. I know, for instance, that the cause of the universe is not a green dragon with red spots living in a cave beneath San Pietro.

I have said that theology speaks in metaphor. Theologians have preferred to say that theological language is analogical, and analogical discourse is not necessarily metaphorical. When we say that God exists and causes, 'exist' and 'cause', they explain, are being used in analogical senses. However; theological attempts to explain how non-metaphorical analogy applies to God have been, in my view, unsuccessful. Scholastic theologians, drawing inspiration from cryptic passages in Aristotle, distinguished two kinds of analogy: analogy of attribution and analogy of proportionality.

Analogy of attribution was often illustrated by reference to the term 'healthy'. Strictly speaking, only living things such as animals and plants can be healthy. But a climate or a complexion may naturally be described as healthy. A climate was healthy, the scholastics explained, because it was a cause of health in animals, the prime analogate; a complexion was healthy because it signified, or was caused by, health in the prime analogate, the human animal. Thus causality was the key to analogy of attribution. But this kind of analogy will not explain the attribution of predicates drawn from creatures to the creator. For in one sense God is the cause of everything (and therefore no one predicate of creatures belongs to him rather than any other) and in another sense, God, standing outside the causal series as *prima causa analoga*, is not the cause of anything.

Analogy of proportionality did not depend on causal relationships. It may be illustrated with reference to the analogous term 'good'. A good knife is a knife that is handy and sharp; a good strawberry is a strawberry that is soft and tasty. Clearly, goodness in knives

is something quite different from goodness in strawberries; yet it does not seem to be a mere pun to call
both knives and strawberries 'good', nor does one
seem to be using a metaphor drawn from knives when
one calls a particular batch of strawberries good. The
explanation of this kind of usage, the scholastics
explained, was a kind of arithmetical proportion, thus:

$$\text{goodness of x} :: \text{essence of x} =$$
$$\text{goodness of y} :: \text{essence of y}.$$

It is because we know the essence of knives and strawberries that we can understand what 'good' means
applied to each of them; without having to learn a
separate lesson in each case.

The difficulty in applying this pattern of analogy in
the case of God is that we have no idea what his essence
is. Even those who have thought that we had, in a fairly
strong sense, a concept of God have fallen short of
saying that we have any grasp of God's essence. So the
analogous predicates which function as, according to
the theory, 'good' does, cannot be applied to God in
any meaningful way, if we insist on literal meaning.

Let us draw a contrast, between metaphor and
analogy. The two concepts are very different, and the
distinction between them is not a matter of a fuzzy
borderline.

Analogy belongs in the realm of sense. A mastery of
the language is enough to convey understanding of the
analogous terms in a language (like 'good' and 'cause') –
indeed a person who did not understand that certain

terms were analogous would not understand their meaning in the language at all.

With metaphor it is different. Metaphor is a movement from one language-game to another. It is not a matter of mastery of a language-game. To introduce a metaphor is not to introduce a new role into a language, to introduce a new sense into the dictionary. Consider a metaphor adapted from Flaubert by Richard Swinburne: 'Human language is a cracked kettle on which we beat our tunes for bears to dance to.'[1] This does not call for the introduction of a new lexical entry under the dictionary heading 'kettle'.

However, a metaphor may become *dead*. It becomes dead when it does enter a new language-game – when it is used, not as an original creative act, nor as an allusion to a famous creative use, but as a part of an independent language-game. Then a new sense is added to the word. The test of when this has happened is this: could you learn the new sense – the new language-game – independently of the original one? The use of 'high' and 'low' in respect of notes on the scale is an example of dead metaphor of this kind.

Metaphor does not belong, then, to the realm of sense or language-game. Does it belong to the realm of speech acts? Not, certainly, in the sense in which stating and commanding are two different speech acts. You can command, no less than describe, in metaphor ('Don't be such a dog in the manger!').

[1] Richard Swinburne, *Revelation: From Metaphor to Analogy* (Oxford: Oxford University Press, 1992), p. 48.

My claim is that theological metaphor is *irreducible*. It can never become dead metaphor, and it can never be replaced by literal language. Consider the sentence 'God wrote his law in the hearts of men.' In this sentence we have three levels of metaphor. The word 'heart' is now a dead metaphor. Any dictionary will include some such sense as 'capacity for feeling emotion'. 'Write' is not in the same case. Literal writing in the heart is, no doubt, possible for a surgeon. Metaphorically, to write something in someone's heart is to bring it about that they are emotionally attached to it. One might say, for, instance, that St Francis wrote his rule in the hearts of his first disciples.

In the case of St Francis, one could describe literally what he did. By his instruction, encouragement, example, he brought it about that his disciples followed his rule with enthusiasm. But when God wrote his law in the hearts of men, what did God do? There is nothing which can be assigned as the way in which he brought it about that the children of Israel loved his law.

Metaphor, as has been said, is not a move in a language-game. It is, in the standard case, taking a word which has a role in one language-game and moving it to another. In the case of God it is taking a word which has no role in any standard language-game and using it in other games. Where names are used in ordinary language-games either the input to the game (experience) or the output (behaviour) involves contact with the object named. With God it is not so; we have no experience of God, and we cannot affect him in any way. If there is such a thing as a religious language-game, it is not a language-game in which there is literal truth.

Having drawn the distinction between metaphor and analogy, let us return to the topic of analogy. Let us set aside Kantian and Wittgensteinian inhibitions and let us speak of the cause of the world. 'X is cause of the world' will certainly not apply to anything but God. If there is a God, it will surely be true of him; so why not say that it is a concept of God?

It is true that cause is an analogous notion. The way in which I cause an uproar is different from the way in which the dropped match causes a fire and gravity causes heavy bodies to fall towards the earth. It is true also, I think, that the notion of cause is an open-ended one; we do not have a closed set of types of causation, and science is forever discovering new kinds of causes, and has long ago abandoned the Cartesian idea that in the material world collision was the only form of agency. So that it would not be an argument against holding that God was the cause of the world to say that we had not the faintest idea what the mode of God's causation was.

But the notion of *cause* is not just an analogous one. It is also something else: let us call it a *heuristic* notion. By a heuristic notion I mean a notion used in order to draw attention to a question to be asked. We can speak of the cause of cancer, of the value of an equation, or the solution to the problems of Northern Ireland without knowing what is the cause, the value or the solution. We can do so sensibly without knowing even how to set about acquiring the relevant knowledge. We can talk about the solution to a problem even in cases where – as perhaps in Northern Ireland – it may turn out that there is no solution.

All heuristic notions, I conjecture, are analogous notions; but the converse is not true: we apply analogous notions in answering questions as well as in demarcating questions to be asked. Now we have two questions to ask about God: is it possible that God can only be talked of in analogous terms? Is it possible that God can only be talked of in heuristic terms? An affirmative answer to the second of these questions is stronger than one to the first – stronger in the sense that it is an even more negative type of theology.

God, the scholastics insisted, is not in any genus; God is not any particular kind of thing, God is a thing of no particular kind. So no generic predicate, no sortal predicate is true of God; or, put another way, '. . . is God' is not a sortal predicate; 'Yahweh is God' is not to be construed as similar to 'Fido is a dog' or 'Peter is human'. With God, there can be neither naming nor specifying; if we are to say anything literally of him at all, it must be by way of description. But how can we describe him if we cannot refer to him; and how can we refer to him if we cannot name or specify him?

The answer at first seems easy: we can refer to him – as we refer to lots of things – by heuristic description. It is, after all, to description, not to naming and specifying, that talk of analogy belongs: it is descriptive predicates, not names or sortal predicates, which can be described as analogous or univocal. There are no analogous names, and no analogous species; and if we can make reference by analogy, it is by using analogous terms in the formulation of a definite description. Similarly with metaphor: a name cannot be metaphorical, and though we can use species-terms metaphorically ('he is a mouse'; 'she is a tiger'), in these cases we are not metaphorically assigning someone to a different species but describing their characteristics by a comparison with the characteristics of different species.

So the problem of how we can talk about God reduces itself to the question whether it is possible to make reference by heuristic description alone. And my answer would be that it is possible to refer to something by a heuristic description only if it is in principle possible to find some other description for it, even if we do not yet know what it is (as the cure for cancer might turn out to be some drug which could be described by its molecular structure, or the solution to the situation in Northern Ireland a set of constitutional arrangements). But theologians seem sometimes perilously close to the view that God can be described by no predicates other than heuristic ones. It is not that we do not know the answers to the questions: 'What kind of thing is God?'; 'What is the mode of divine causality?' It is that no answers are possible in principle.

The predicates which religious people apply to God can be divided into two classes. There are bodily predicates, and these seem to be almost universally agreed to be metaphorical. There are mentalistic predicates, and these would be claimed by at least some theologians to be literally true of God. Being literally true does not of course prevent a predicate from being analogical: consider the analogical nature of a verb like 'love': loving chocolates involves wanting to eat them, loving my mother-in-law does not involve wanting to eat her, and so on.

Mentalistic predicates are used primarily of human beings; they are ascribed to human beings on the basis of their behaviour. We do not ascribe mentalistic properties and mental acts only to human beings: we ascribe them also to animals who behave in ways similar to human beings. We also ascribe mental acts and processes to human institutions and artefacts: to governments, say, to texts and to computers. This is not because governments and texts and computers behave like human beings, but because of the relationships they have to the humans who constitute them, create them, use them. If we try to ascribe mentality to God we cannot do so in any of these ways. God has no behaviour to resemble human behaviour in the way animal behaviour does; he is not, if he really is a God, a human creation like a government, a text or a computer.

The language-games in which mentalistic predicates have their home are games which can only be played with respect to human beings and things that resemble human beings. It is for this reason that I have claimed that we cannot speak literally about God.

When I say that we speak of God in metaphor, I am not, of course, saying: 'There is a God, who has such and such properties, and one of his properties is that he can be spoken of only metaphorically.' I mean that any sentence in which the word 'God' appears has an irreducibly metaphorical content. This does not mean that it is trivial, or unimportant, or that it should not have any consequences for our own fundamental attitudes. It may well be that the use of such metaphors is essential if we are to have a proper understanding of the world in which we live. But the metaphorical nature of religious language does mean that it is profoundly mysterious: more mysterious than any theory of analogical predication can really allow. For it means that when we talk in the language of the divine metaphor, we do not really know what the metaphors are about.

4

God and Mind

Is there a personal God? No doubt that depends on what you mean by 'personal' and what you mean by 'God'. Let us assume, with regard to persons, that whatever else it may be, a person is something which can know and love. Let us assume, with regard to God, that whatever else God may be, God is immaterial and infinite. Then the question whether there is a personal God can be answered in the affirmative only if these attributes – knowledge, love, immateriality and infinity – are compatible with each other.

Instead of asking whether there is a personal God, we might ask whether there is a God who has a mind. This may, indeed, be a clearer question to pose. In the context of theology the notion of 'person' is a complicated one. According to the Christian doctrine of the incarnation, for instance, a single person may be both human and divine, both man and God. According to the Christian doctrine of the Trinity, three distinct persons may be one single God. To avoid entangling ourselves in these doctrinal complications, let us pose the simpler question: is there a divine mind?

But what is a mind? A correct, but unenlightening, answer is this: a mind is an intellect plus a will. The intellect and the will, according to a long philosophical tradition, are the two great faculties of the mind. The intellect is the locus, or home, of knowledge, and the will is the locus, or home, of love. So the question whether there is such a thing as a divine mind rests, once again, on the question whether the attributes of knowledge and love are compatible with the other attributes of divinity.

The things which we attempt to say about God are, in some obvious sense, tied up with the things which we human beings say about each other. If we are interested in whether God is a person it is because personal relationships have a unique importance for human beings. When we speak of God's knowledge and love we are using words which we feel most at home in using about ourselves and our fellow humans. The minds which we know best – perhaps the only ones about which we have real knowledge – are human minds.

Is it correct to say that all our notions of divinity are derived from our notions of humanity? Some philosophers have argued that the relationship of derivation goes in the other direction. The notions which we apply in describing human states of mind and mental acts, they maintain, have their primary application to a superhuman mind. Thus Descartes – while still in doubt about the existence of the external world, and while longing to achieve basic certainty – argues for the existence of God in the following terms: 'How could I understand my doubting and desiring – that is, my lacking something and not being altogether perfect – if I had no idea of a more perfect being as a standard by which to recognize my own defects?' For Descartes, my consciousness of my own imperfect knowledge and unsatisfied love in some sense depends on a conception of the perfect knowledge and love which is God's.

Other philosophers have thought that the paradigm of knowledge is the information acquired by human beings through the use of their bodily senses, and the paradigm of love is the affection expressed by human beings through their bodily behaviour. Thus Wittgenstein insisted that the language-games which provide the environment for mentalistic predicates are language-games grafted on to human forms of life. 'Only of a human being and what resembles (behaves like) a living human being can one say: it has sensations; it sees; is blind; hears; is deaf; is conscious or unconscious.'[1]

Both Descartes and Wittgenstein think that in using mental predicates we begin by applying them to human beings; but Descartes takes as his paradigm the application of these predicates by a single human being to himself in the secrecy of his own mind; Wittgenstein takes as his paradigm the application of these predicates to a third person by members of a common language-using community.

[1] Ludwig Wittgenstein, *Philosophical Investigations* (Oxford: Blackwell, 1953).

Descartes was a dualist: that is to say, he believed that in addition to the world of matter there was a separate world of mind. This mental world was accessible only to introspection: and the meanings of the predicates which applied within this mental world must be learned by each person by an inward look at the contents of a private realm. In sharp reaction to Descartes there grew up in the twentieth century the theory of behaviourism, which denied the existence of the mental realm. According to the behaviourists, when we attribute mental states or acts to people we are really making statements about their actual or hypothetical bodily behaviour: behaviour in the one and only world of matter.

Wittgenstein proposed a philosophy of mind which was a middle stance between behaviourism and Cartesian dualism. Mental events and states, he believed, were neither reducible to their bodily expressions (as the behaviourists believed) nor totally separable from them (as Descartes had believed). According to him the connection between mental and physical states is neither one of logical reduction (as in behaviourist theory) nor one of causal connection (as in Cartesian theory). According to him the physical expression of a mental process is a *criterion* for that process; that is to say, it is part of the concept of a mental process of a particular kind that it should have a characteristic manifestation. The criteria by which we attribute states of mind and mental acts, Wittgenstein showed, are bodily states and activities.

In my view, which I have defended in several other

49

books, Wittgenstein's account provides the most rewarding context for the pursuit of questions in the philosophy of mind. If this is so, then there is a problem for those who wish to talk of a divine mind. How can mentality be attributed to a being like the God of tradition who is totally immaterial and non-bodily? This problem will be the main topic of this and the following essay.

If we accept the Wittgensteinian position that the meaning of terms for the inner life is given by outward criteria of bodily behaviour, there remains the question: what is the criterion, or set of criteria, by which we draw the distinction between mind and body altogether? Even if it is to bodies primarily that we attribute minds, we do not attribute minds to all bodies. On what basis do we make the distinction between those bodies to which we attribute minds and those to which we do not attribute minds? We have spoken of 'mentalistic predicates', meaning predicates which imply the having of a mind, predicates appropriate to entities with minds. How do we decide which predicates *are* mentalistic in this sense?

We can approach this question from two different directions. Because the mind is both intellect and will, we may enquire what are the criteria on the basis of which we attribute intellect and intellectual activity; or we may enquire what are the criteria on the basis of which we attribute will and volitional activity. The intellect is the cognitive side of the mind, and the will is the affective side of the mind. So our enquiry, in its twofold form, can be rephrased thus: what are the criteria on the basis of which we attribute cognitive and affective states of mind?

Cognitive states of mind are those which involve the possession of a piece of information (true or false): such things as consciousness, awareness, expectation, belief, certainty, knowledge. Affective states of mind are neither true nor false but consist in an attitude of pursuit or avoidance: such things as purpose, intention, desire, volition, dislike, disgust, love. Accordingly, criteria of mentality may be criteria of cognitivity (criteria for the attribution of cognitive states) or criteria of affectivity (criteria for the attribution of affective states).

If we start on the cognitive side, one way of answering our question is to identify mind with consciousness. We may say that those beings have minds which have consciousness; or that what goes on in my mind, as opposed to what goes on in my body, is that of which I am immediately conscious.

Another way of making the distinction between mind and body is to say that the mind is interior, the body exterior. There are, it may be said, two worlds: the mental and the physical. The external, physical, world is something which is common to all of us; the internal, mental, world is something which is private to each of us; or perhaps we should rather say that there are as many different internal worlds as there are minds.

There are different ways of drawing the distinction between mind and body, ways which make a close link between mind and language. Some philosophers say that the only beings that have minds are those that make use of language. Others would draw the distinction within the realm of language itself. Languages may be conceivable, they would say, which would not be evidence of minds on the part of those which use them – languages, perhaps, like the language of the bees. Mentality must be sought, according to this view, in a particular feature of the languages with which we are familiar. This feature, called by some philosophers intentionality, is the ability to talk about the non-existent, and to use different, non-synonymous ways of speaking about the same existent objects. Some philosophers identify intentionality, in this sense, as the mark of the mental; and considerable philosophical effort has been expended in seeking to give a rigorous, formal, account of such intentionality.

Intentionality may be used as a criterion of the mental in two distinct but connected ways. One may claim that only the use of a language which involved intentionality is sufficient evidence for mentality on the part of its user. Or one may claim that only a language which involved intentionality would be rich enough to enable a speaker to make attributions of mental states and activities. Both claims, of course, may be true together.

For some philosophers the essential feature of mentality is not intentionality but rationality: the ability to give and understand reasons. Intentionality, on this view, is a necessary but not a sufficient condition for rationality. On this view the tradition was soundly inspired which defined human beings not as language-using animals, nor even as intentional language-using animals, but as rational animals.

Some philosophers have set their sights even higher, and taken as the mark of the mind not mere rationality but spirituality. By 'spirituality' here I do not mean any kind of existence apart from a body, but merely the ability to consider matters lying beyond the spatial and temporal limits of the individual's bodily life and experience. For philosophers of this kind, even the most rational management of one's daily business would not be a manifestation of mind. Mind is to be seen in the mathematician's study of unending series, the cosmologist's speculation on the origin of the universe, the monk's meditation on the infinite.

Such are various ways in which philosophers have characterized the mind by appeal to different kinds of cognitive ability and performance. One may seek, on the other hand, to use affective rather than cognitive criteria to single out what, from among the operation of the myriad different kinds of agents in the universe, is the kind of behaviour which is the mark of the mental.

Not everything that happens in the universe is a case of agency: in addition to what things do there is what happens to them. If I hit a cricket ball into a rosebush, that is an action of mine, but it is only something that happens to the ball and the bush. The movements of the planets are not any acting out of the planets' nature; they are the result of the application to the planets of laws of motion of a very general kind. Or if we are to call gravitational attraction a form of agency, then we may say that the movement of the planets is the result of the agency of many massy bodies scatttered through the cosmos. It is not to be attributed to the planets' own agency, in the way in which ancient and medieval philosophers and poets believed.

None the less, agency is a universal phenomenon, not restricted to human or living beings. The corrosive action of acid and the budding of a hawthorn are examples of agency no less than a dolphin's swimming or the knitting of a sweater. Since there are both animate and inanimate agents, agency by itself is not a mark of life, still less of mind. The difference between animate and inanimate agency seems to be that animate agency, unlike inanimate agency, is teleological agency: it is action in pursuit of goals. Thus living beings, unlike non-living ones, frequently act in order to bring about some benefit to themselves or their kind, as we see in the life-cycles of plants and even simpler organisms.

Even among living agents, there is a difference between the kind of agency typical of plants, on the one hand, and that typical of animals and human beings on the other. Natural agency is common to all living beings, but voluntary agency is to be found only in animals. While plants and animals both have needs, only animals have wants or desires, and voluntary action in animals is acting out of desire.

Human beings, like animals, have desires; but human beings can want things which no animal could want – to be richer than Croesus, for instance, or to be famous after one's death. One reason for the difference between human and animal wanting is that human beings can have wants which can only be expressed in language. Humans and animals can both perform voluntary actions, but only humans can perform intentional actions, that is, actions done with the consciousness of why one is doing them. Intentional action, therefore, may be taken as one criterion of mentality.

In the affective realm, as in the cognitive realm, some philosophers wish to assign more exalted criteria of mentality. Some might wish to argue that it is not the ordinary, self-regarding intentional actions that are the true mark of the human possession of mind. It is rather the pursuit of altruistic and self-transcending goals which is the emblem of the human spirit: loving one's neighbour, working for the millennium, seeking scientific understanding, loving God.

The affective and cognitive items which we have listed are not two independent sets of criteria for mentality. If they were, it would be hard to see why we should talk of the mind as a single entity at all. In fact, at every level cognitive and affective are interwoven. Animal desire and animal consciousness go together: the notions of wanting and of awareness become applicable to an agent together, when the agent's behaviour manifests the requisite degree of complexity. If we know an animal's capacities, its behavioural repertoire, we can infer its goals from its behaviour if we know what elements of its environment it is aware of; and we can infer from its behaviour what elements of its environment it is aware of if we know what goals it is pursuing. At the other end of the scale, the pursuit of transcendent spiritual goals is possible only for those who have the appropriate concepts to formulate such goals. Will is impossible without intellect. But equally, though in a less obvious manner, intellect is impossible without will: what is sublime cannot be understood without a degree of sympathy for what makes it sublime.

I have listed various characteristics which may be taken, and have been taken by some philosophers, as being crucial tokens of the presence of mind. The rest of this essay will indeed be devoted to developing, and evaluating, the criteria, with a view to deciding how, if at all, the most appropriate criteria for mentality can be applied to a being who possessed the other attributes of divinity.

If we take consciousness as the mark of mind, then we must say that not only human beings, but also some animals, have minds. For there is no doubt that apes and horses and cows and cats and dogs and rats and mice are conscious, if to be conscious means to see and hear and smell and taste, and so on. Descartes, who was the first philosopher systematically to define mind in terms of consciousness, denied that animals had minds because he denied that they were conscious; but in this he was wrong. He was correct in believing that animals do not possess self-consciousness in the way that human beings do: animals do not possess the concept which human beings manifest in their use of the first-person pronoun. But self-consciousness is not the same thing as consciousness, and consciousness – in the form of sense-perception – is possible in the absence of self-consciousness.

On the other hand, if we define mind in terms of the exalted spiritual activities in which some philosophers have placed its essence then we seem in danger of having to say that not all human beings have minds. For it is not immediately obvious that all human beings have the ability to be scientists, poets, metaphysicians or mystics. Perhaps it might turn out that all human beings, given appropriate training, are capable of understanding the most sublime thoughts capable of expression in human language. Even so, it does not seem impossible that there might be other beings, inhabitants perhaps of distant galaxies, who could master the everyday use of our natural languages, but were baffled whenever these languages were employed in fundamental scientific research or put to poetical or metaphysical or religious use.

This essay and the next will be devoted to refining a definition of mind with a view to seeing how far the notion of mind can be extended, and in particular if it can be applied to a divine being. As a starting point for the enquiry, I will take as a working definition that to have a mind is to have an intellect and a will. In the case of a human being, to have an intellect is to have the capacity to acquire and exercise intellectual abilities of various kinds, such as the mastery of language and the possession of objective information. In the case of a human being, to have a will is to have the capacity for the free pursuit of goals formulated by the intellect.

In human beings, the mind is a capacity, somethinig potential: intellectual skills are not always being exercised, not every moment of life is spent in the pursuit of rational goals. Babies have minds even though they have not yet acquired the language which will permit them to exercise intellectual and volitional activity. If we are to attribute mind to a God who is unchangeable and in whom there is no distinction between potentiality and actuality, then we must be prepared to accept that these features of the human mind are due to its humanity and not to its mentality. The contrast is sometimes made by theologians in the following terms: you and I *have* minds, but God *is* a mind.

If the human mind is a capacity, what is it a capacity *of*? Of the living human organism. It is wrong to think that human beings are somehow composed of bodies and minds; they are bodies that have minds. Stones and trees are bodies (i.e. corporeal objects) which do not have minds; men and women are bodies which do have minds. Cats and dogs are bodies which have minds on some definitions of mind, and not on others. On the definition just given, cats and dogs do not have minds because they do not have the ability to acquire language.

A capacity is a kind of ability: it is a second-order ability, an ability to acquire abilities. (Speaking Russian is an activity; knowing Russian is an ability; having the ability to learn Russian is a capacity.) In the human case we must distinguish between the possessor of the capacity (the human being) and the capacity itself (the mind). In the divine case, we will have to meet the contention that there is no distinction between mind and possessor.

Abilities need to be distinguished not only from their possessors but from their exercises and their vehicles. Where an ability is the ability to do X, then actually doing X is the exercise of that ability. The vehicle of an ability is the physical ingredient or structure in virtue of which an ability belongs to its possessor. Two examples will bring out the nature of these distinctions and their importance. Knowing Russian, which is an ability, is clearly distinct from actually speaking Russian, which is one of the activities which are exercises of that ability: I may know Russian even though I am fast asleep and uttering no sound. Being able to prevent colds, which again is an ability, is distinct from the property of containing vitamin C, though vitamin C is the vehicle of the prophylactic power of my winter pills. No doubt the possession of the power is causally connected with the containing of the vitamin, but cause and effect are two distinct things here.

The distinction between abilities and their vehicles is an important one in the context of the mind. The vehicle of the human mind is no doubt the brain and central nervous system. If abilities were identical with their vehicles, then the notion of a disembodied mind would be an impossible one from the start. But because the link between an ability and its vehicle may be an empirical, contingent one, then it needs examination whether the mind might not continue to exist without the appropriate vehicle. And in the case of a God who has no body, we must ask whether the mind could exist without any vehicle at all.

Because the human mind is a capacity, an ability, philosophical misunderstanding of the nature of abilities can lead to confusion in the philosophy of mind. Someone who confuses abilities with their exercises will be a behaviourist: she will identify the mind with its behavioural exercise. Someone who confuses abilities with their vehicles will be a materialist: he will identify the mind with its material vehicle in the brain. Both errors in philosophical psychology have their root in a defective metaphysic of ability.

The mind, we said, consists of the intellect and the will. But if the mind is not a physical substance, how can it have parts? Can it have a structure at all, if it is not a concrete object? Yes, provided that it is understood that when we speak of parts and structure here we are talking about relationships that hold between different abilities, and not about relationships holding between material objects. There is a relationship between the ability to play chess and the ability to move the knight correctly: the latter is clearly a part of the former. But neither ability is a divisible physical entity.

A consideration of the sense in which the mind is divisible into parts is of importance in the context of our present enquiry, since one of the attributes which theologians have traditionally ascribed to God is that of being simple, of lacking any partition or divisibility. If we are to establish the coherence of a divine mind, we must enquire whether divine simplicity is compatible with the kind of structure which appears to be characteristic of anything we could call a mind.

The human minds we know are embodied minds, material and finite, which develop over time, which enquire, learn, forget and err. In this section are to enquire whether there can be a mind which is immaterial, infinite, unchanging, incurious and unerring, which learns nothing and forgets nothing. Since the minds we know best are human minds, it may be that there is an unavoidable degree of anthropomorphism in attributing minds to any beings, finite or infinite, which are not human. But must anthropomorphism necessarily lead to nonsense? The next essay will be an attempt to explore the logical limits of anthropomorphism.

5

The Limits of Anthropomorphism

Anthropomorphism does not occur only in the context of theism. From time to time we take predicates that are strictly applicable only to human beings and apply them to things other than human beings. We use them, for instance, of parts of human beings, of animals and of machines of various kinds.

Human beings, like other animals, breathe, digest their food and grasp other bodies. We can speak, by synecdoche, of organic parts as performing these activities: our lungs breathe, our stomachs digest, our hands grasp. This usage, though metaphorical, is generally philosophically harmless. But it can be dangerous to speak of parts of the body as performing mental activities which only a whole human being can perform. When I see the Matterhorn, there are images on my retina and there are specific events in my visual cortex. But neither my retina nor my visual cortex sees the Matterhorn, and no part of me sees my retinal images or my visual cortex. These truisms are sometimes forgotten by practising psychologists.

Descartes, who was one of the first to explore the nature of retinal images, warned us not to think that there was another pair of eyes inside our brains to see the images. But his own account of seeing – as a perception, by the mind, of patterns in the pineal gland – was itself tantamount to postulating a homunculus or little human at the innermost point of the brain. Psychologists in our own time have not been immune to the illusion that the cognitive and affective activities of human beings can be explained by the postulation of mythical cognitive or affective activities to be performed by organic or microscopic parts of human beings. To avoid being misled here, it is wise to be most cautious in attributing human psychological predicates to human parts less than the whole human being.

The attribution of human predicates to animals is a more serious and complicated matter. We can sum up the issue in the age-old question: Do animals think? Descartes maintained that animals did not think, and did not have minds. In order to decide how far he was right and how far he was wrong, we have to distinguish various things which might be meant by saying that animals do not think.

First, it may mean that animals do not have Cartesian consciousness: they do not have private ideas or thoughts with which they are immediately acquainted and which are the medium of their contact with the world outside them. If this is what is meant by saying that animals do not think, then the thesis is a true one.

But it is also an uninteresting one, because if this is what 'think' means then human beings do not think either. We do not have Cartesian consciousness any more than animals do, because Cartesian consciousness is a nonsensical *Unding*.

Secondly, it may mean that animals are machines, that their behaviour is susceptible to mechanistic explanation, and that there is not, in the make-up of an animal, any room for an immaterial substance. We may agree that there is no immaterial animal ego: but yet we may also query whether there is an immaterial human ego, and we may regard it as an open question whether human behaviour itself may not be susceptible to mechanistic explanation.

Thirdly, it may mean that animals cannot use language: they do not have the species-specific ability for language-learning, which is something distinct from general intelligence. Descartes certainly maintained this, and in our own time it has been defended by Chomsky; it has also been controverted by many animal behaviourists, some of whom have claimed that specially trained chimpanzees have actually mastered human language.

I do not wish to enter into the question whether only human beings, among terrestrial animals, have the power to master human languages. The reports I have read of the performances of chimpanzees such as Washoe and Sarah and their successors have not convinced me that these gifted animals have genuine linguistic skills. But it is a matter of empirical research to discover how far non-human animals can be trained to use human languages. What I am concerned with is rather the philosophical question about the relationship between mind and language in animals. This is not so much the question whether animals have minds but rather the question whether 'dumb' animals (the 'brute beasts' of the older terminology) have minds.

The question whether animals have minds is, *pace* Descartes, a different question from the question whether they think. Thinking is an activity or a state, whereas mind is a capacity; and thinking covers more different kinds of activity than the activity the mind is a capacity for. I have argued earlier that the mind is the capacity to acquire intellectual abilities, that is to say the ability for intellectual activities. If intellectual activities are those which involve the creation and utilization of symbols, then dumb animals do not have minds, because they do not, as we do, create and use symbols. But that does not settle the question whether they think.

Animals are undoubtedly conscious agents. Even inanimate bodies and feelingless plants are capable of agency; *a fortiori* animals are agents. Unlike stones and trees, animals are conscious in the sense that they are capable of perception and sensation: they see, hear, feel pain and hunger and thirst. There is nothing anthropomorphic in attributing sense-perception to animals, and we are not using metaphor if we speak of the eye of a bird or a fish.

Descartes denied that animals were conscious or possessed sensation in the truest sense. He would only allow that there was sensation where there were sense-data. The fact that animals had the appropriate mechanisms in their bodies, analogous to our organs of sight, hearing, taste and smell, was insufficient to make it true that they could really perceive with their senses. We may agree that the mere presence of the appropriate mechanism for perception and sensation is not enough: a human brain, with the appropriate nerves attached, if removed from the body and placed *in vitro*, cannot see or hear or smell. But the animal mechanism is not *in vitro*, it is in an animal organism, and the organism as a whole can react and behave in the appropriate way to display the various modes of awareness of the environment characteristic of the different senses.

Animals have simple beliefs and desires; we attribute these to them on the basis of their behaviour, powers and needs. When we attribute beliefs and desires to animals, we make use of the indirect speech construction as we do in the case of human beings: we say of a dog, for instance, that he thinks that he is going to be taken for a walk, or that he wants his master to open the door for him. This does not mean that we believe dogs have some canine language in which to think and want; but it does mean that we are attributing to them such concepts as are implied in our ascription of belief and desire. Belief and desire are dispositional concepts, and we specify what dispositions are by describing what would count as an exercise of the disposition. If no difference can be made out between an agent's expressing that p and expressing that q, then we cannot make a distinction in the case of that agent between the belief that p and the belief that q, or the wish that p were the case and the wish that q were the case.

In speech-using human beings the possession of a concept of X involves two things: (1) being able to recognize an X for an X, react to it appropriately in behaviour, etc.; (2) being able to use a symbol for an X. (In most cases it is difficult or impossible to get a fine exact point of behaviour to fit X and X alone, other than a linguistic one). In dumb animals there is only the first of these abilities. But this is enough to say that animals do have concepts of certain things, for instance a dog may have the appropriate concepts for the recognition of other dogs, of his mistress, of food, etc. We do not need to say that a dog has the same concepts as we have when we talk of the dog's mistress, but only that he possesses a concept which enables him to pick out the object which we pick out when we speak of his mistress. Even in the case of human beings, we sometimes use, in the attribution of beliefs, concepts which are possessed by us rather than by the believer: as when we say that King Henry VIII was worried about inflation.

There is nothing necessarily anthropomorphic in attributing concepts to animals. Anthropomorphism comes out only if we attribute to them concepts whose possession can only be manifested in language. In the case of human beings, there are some concepts whose possession involves only the second of the two abilities mentioned above: for instance, the concept of a million, or of yesterday, or of 'if . . . then'. It is in these cases that it is difficult to allow the possession of the concepts to dumb animals.

The distinction between those concepts which it makes sense to attribute to animals and those which it does not has been made by Frege and by Wittgenstein.

Frege, discussing the idea of some philosophers that number one is the property of being undivided and isolated, has this to say:

> If this were correct, then we should have to expect animals, too, to be capable of having some sort of idea of unity. Can it be that a dog staring at the moon does have an idea, however ill-defined, of what we signify by the word 'one'? This is hardly credible – and yet it certainly distinguishes individual objects: another dog, its master, a stone it is playing with, these certainly appear to the dog every bit as isolated, as self-contained, as undivided, as they do to us. It will notice a difference, no doubt, between being set on by several other dogs and being set on by only one, but this is what Mill calls the physical difference. We need to know specifically: is the dog conscious, however dimly, of that common element in the two situations which we express by the word 'one', when, for example, it first is bitten by one larger dog and then chases one cat. This seems to me unlikely.[1]

Wittgenstein said:

> One can imagine an animal angry, frightened, unhappy, happy, startled. But hopeful? And why not?
>
> A dog believes his master is at the door. But can he also

[1] Frege, *The Foundations of Arithmetic* (Oxford: Blackwell, 1953), p. 41.

believe his master will come the day after tomorrow? – And what can he not do here? – how do I do it? How am I supposed to answer this?

Can only those hope who can talk? Only those who have mastered the use of a language. That is to say, the phenomena of hope are modes of this complicated form of life.[2]

Wittgenstein seems to me to have gone wrong here. It is correct that the dog cannot believe that his master will come the day after tomorrow: but the problem is not that the dog cannot hope, but that the dog has no mastery of the calendar. If the dog sees me putting meat and meal into his bowl, and leaps excitedly up and down, there is no reason to deny that he hopes he is about to be fed. Animals can have simple hopes as they can have simple beliefs.

Frege's point, however, seems to be well taken and is capable of application to cases other than that of number. An animal, lacking language, cannot have concepts corresponding to the logical constants (e.g. 'not' and 'if . . . then'). Of course an animal can tell the difference between the state of affairs when it is raining and the state of affairs when it is not raining; and an animal may know that if it does not come when it is called, then it will be beaten. But it has no concept of anything in common to all the cases where we use 'not' or 'if . . . then'.

[2] Ludwig Wittgenstein, *Philosophical Investigations* (Oxford: Blackwell, 1953), p. 174.

Animals don't – if we exclude the dubious cases of the highly trained chimpanzees – reason. The ground for saying that they do not reason is that they do not operate a system of symbols adequate for the giving and evaluation of reasons. Of course animals act for the sake of goals, and do one thing for the sake of another; but unless an animal has a language it cannot act for a reason. A dog may scratch beneath a bush to get at a buried bone. His scratching manifests his desire to get at the bone, but there is nothing in his behaviour to express, over and above this, that he is scratching because he wants to get at the bone. Animals do not have, because they cannot give, reasons for action.

This is not to deny that they make fine, purposive adjustments of behaviour. So do we when we ride a bicycle, but learning to keep one's balance on a bicycle is not a matter of reasoning. It is not just that we do not run through syllogisms in our mind before we make minute changes to the angle of the handlebars: we hardly ever syllogize in that way even in our most reasoned behaviour. In most cases one does not give reasons for one's action, to others or even to oneself: but if one's actions are reasoned actions, one can give the reasons on request. This is not so in the case of the spontaneous movements we make to keep upright on two wheels.

If a rational animal is an animal capable of giving, having and acting upon reasons, then tradition is correct in saying that only humans are rational animals.

Animals, I insisted earlier, are conscious beings. But we must make a distinction between consciousness and self-consciousness. A being is self-conscious if it has a concept equivalent to the mastery of the first-person pronoun in natural human language. Self-consciousness is not possible without language. For a language-user, there is a difference between being in pain and having the thought 'I'm in pain'; outside language there is no room for such a distinction to be made. Frege's point holds again: a pig may feel hungry, but has no concept of that which is in common to his being hungry and his being bloated.

We have agreed that animals lack intellect and will, but have simple beliefs and desires. Do they possess imagination? In one sense of the word, animals can certainly imagine things. We sometimes use the word 'imagine' to record malfunctions of perception: I thought I heard a knock at the door, but I only imagined it; there isn't really a drop there, but the psychologists' visual cliff makes you imagine one; this drug makes you imagine you are moving forward at high speed. There is no reason to deny that animals may imagine things in this sense – though it is a matter of empirical enquiry to discover which (for example) optical illusions they are vulnerable to. But the interesting question about animals is whether they can do what we do when we voluntarily let our imagination wander. Do they imagine things in that sense?

Descartes allowed that they did; but this was because he conceived the imagination as being the capacity for producing images in the brain, and there was no reason to deny that there might be physical images in animals' brains just as there were, according to him, physical images in humans' brains. But the imagination is surely the capacity for mental imagery, not for cerebral imagery. And do animals have imagination in this sense?

If we think of mental images as being some less vivid version of sense impressions there seems no reason to deny imagination to animals. We have agreed that animals have genuine sensation: if we allow them the capacity for vivid impressions, why not the capacity for less vivid ones? But the matter is more complicated than that.

The having of mental images, like other inner processes, is something that needs an outer criterion. We find out about each other's mental images by listening to descriptions of them. In the human case the criterion for the occurrence of mental images is linguistic. Moreover, our ability to have mental images is closely bound up with our ability to talk to ourselves. Even the most fanatical animal-lover will hardly claim that animals have a language which they use only in interior monologue.

However, not all mental imagery, even in our case, is linguistic. Not everything I see in my mind's eye is written matter; not every sound I hear in my mind's ear is spoken words. Why may not dogs smell in their mind's nose, and birds sing in their mind's throat?

The question misses the full force of the claim that an inner process needs an outer criterion. In the human case, linguistic testimony is the criterion not only for the occurrence but for the content of a mental image. When someone tells us what she dreamed or what she imagined, then what she says is decisive: there is no room for the misreporting of mental images by their possessor. If a report is confused, or incoherent, that does not mean that there has been a failure of interior observation: it means that the image itself is hazy or chimeric. If we say, then, that animals may have what we have when we have mental images, what we are suggesting is that they may have something which has an intrinsic relationship to its expression in language, without having any language in which to express it.

But might it not be possible to discover that events took place in animals' brains which were exactly similar to what goes on in our brains when we have mental images? And would not that prove that they too have mental images? In response to these questions we must put a question in return. What does 'exactly similar' mean in this context?

If an event in a human brain is to be any kind of plausible candidate for being the counterpart to a mental image, it has to be an event which is linked in some systematic way to the mental events which would constitute the linguistic expression of the image, since this expression has an intrinsic relation to the image itself. If the purported equivalent in the animal brain lacks this linkage, then it is not 'exactly similar' to the human brain event in the relevant respect. On the other hand, if an event is exactly similar in this respect, then it cannot take place in the brain of an organism which lacks the capacity for linguistic expression.

The question whether any animals can have imagination, therefore, seems in the end to come down to the question whether there are any animals capable of acquiring a language. If we restrict ourselves to the dumb animals with which we are familiar, the question does not seem to have been given a clear sense, for we have not been given a coherent account of what mental imagery is in the absence of any means of its expression.

In the final part of this essay I turn to the third most widespread form of anthropomorphism outside the religious context, namely the application of mentalistic predicates to machines. This has become more wide-spread and more important as more and more people become habituated to using computers; and the more user-friendly computers become, the more natural it is to apply to them predicates (like 'friendly' itself) primarily attributable to human beings.

We speak of computers as calculating, spelling, writing poems, composing music, playing chess. I was once able to observe the behaviour of an early optical scanner, which had shown itself well able to read Latin and Greek founts, faced for the first time with linked-up Arabic script. I found myself spontaneously saying that it was weeping quietly to itself in a corner. This was obviously an instance of the sentimental fallacy. But was it really any more metaphorical than saying that the scanner had *read* the Latin and Greek texts?

We are all familiar with debates in which the intelligence of computers is compared with that of human beings. Partisans of computers argue that computers already outclass human beings in many areas of intellectual endeavour, and will eventually outclass them in all, and perhaps take over the running of the planet. Partisans on the other side will often set up some bound which, they will claim, computers will never pass: computers will never be able to see a joke, to write a novel, to compose a convincing love poem, to understand theology. Whenever the challenge is given an operational definition, the computers usually meet it (commonly some years, or decades, after the computer partisans have predicated that they would).

In these contests, in my view, the partisans of the human race start off on the wrong foot. They should never have accepted the premise that in some areas computers already match human intelligent performance, and look to the future for the barrier which will prevent the computers from taking control. They should point out that computers have, in the literal sense, no intelligence whatsoever. In the literal sense, they cannot perform even the simplest intellectual tasks, like adding two numbers together. Computers can do addition and subtraction only in the same sense as an hour-glass can tell the time. An hour-glass can tell the time in the sense that it is a mechanical device which assists human beings in telling the time; but of course an hour-glass cannot tell the time in any literal sense, having no concept whatever of what time is. A computer, in an exactly parallel way, can add and subtract in the sense that it is an electronic device which assists human beings in adding and subtracting; but it does not have a life of its own in which arithmetic can play the role which it does in our life. The fact that a computer is an immensely more complicated artefact than an hour-glass should not be allowed to obscure the fundamental philosophical point.

In the previous essay the human mind was defined as the capacity for intellectual activity, that is to say, activities involving the creation and utilization of symbols. Computers do not have minds like ours because they lack this capacity. They do, in a sense, operate with symbols; but the symbols are our symbols. The symbols which they use are not symbols for them; it is we and not the computers which confer the meaning on the symbols.

To insist that in the literal sense no intellectual predicate is true of a computer is not to reject the use of anthropomorphism in the relation between user and computer. It is natural, and perhaps unavoidable, for a user to attribute thoughts and purposes to her computer; indeed doing so may positively assist the user in getting the most out of the computer with which she is dealing. This is because the software which she is using is itself a fruit of human intelligence. Whatever a piece of software does is the execution of an intention, however conditional and remote, of the programmer who wrote it. (Of course the programmer does not know how his intentions are going to be executed, in fact; any more than does the terrorist who places the bomb in the railway station waste-bin. None the less, the running of the software and the maiming of the victim are executions of intention in each case.) Computers are not competitors with, but extensions of, human intelligence and volition.

It is time to draw the moral from these reflections on

anthropomorphism, and ask how the criteria that we use for applying mental predicates could be applied to a being that was divine. If the scope for extending the use of such predicates to animals and machines is as limited as we have seen, there must be a much greater difficulty in extending them to God. Animals and machines are like human beings in important ways: they are bodily objects, they have parts, they have histories. The distance is infinitely greater between a human and a God who is immaterial, uncomplex, unchanging.

It is difficult enough to conceive even of a finite mind without a body. Some of our mental operations, such as sensation and emotion, are intimately linked with bodily organs and bodily reactions. The traditional teaching of Christian theologians was that such operations were impossible without a body: disembodied minds can neither see nor hear nor feel pain and anger. Secular philosophical reflection, in this area, reaches the same conclusion as theological tradition.

But what of pure intellectual thought – may that not be possible without a body? We must first ask what thought consists in. Thought involves activities of many different kinds: of the body, of the senses, of the imagination. What makes these activities deserve the name 'intellectual' is the control that is exercised over them. But keeping something under control is not itself an activity, any more than keeping one's balance on a bicycle is. So the notion of a pure intellectual activity remains obscure.

Of course, we all think many thoughts that we do

not express by any outward words or movements of our bodies. We utter them to ourselves, perhaps, in the secrecy of the imagination. But the imagination is itself linked to the body, in the sense that the criterion for *what* we imagine is what we would report in the public language of our social life – the only language we have. The imagination is one possible medium of thought, a medium in the sense that there are vocal and manual media of speech.

It is a remarkable fact about the intellect that there are no limits (other than formal ones of a necessary level of mathematical complexity) upon the medium in which its activities can be expressed. Any particular bodily medium is therefore dispensable. But it does not follow that thought is possible in the absence of any bodily medium whatsoever.

Any thought has a content and a possessor: it is a thought *of* something, and it is *somebody*'s thought. How do we individuate the possessor of a thought? In the normal case, by looking to the body that expresses the thought. Content alone will not individuate the possessor of a thought: many other people have the same thoughts that I have. Content only individuates when it includes reference to modes of individuation of thoughts other than by their content (e.g. appeals to the bodily history of the thinker of the thought, or to the normal information-gathering capacities of human beings). Even in alleged cases of telepathy or spirit-possession, physical criteria come into play, explicitly or implicitly, in the ascription of an expressed thought to an individual thinker.

It is perhaps barely possible to conceive of a dis-embodied spirit which is individuated not by having a body but by having an individual locus or viewpoint on the world. By this I mean that we imagine it as possessing information which, in the case of a normal embodied mind, would be available only from a particular point in space and time. This limited viewpoint would mark off an individual of this kind from other possible such disembodied entities. The viewpoint would thus find expression in the content of the thoughts entertained by such a being. The being could be tracked, one might say, as an information centre. Such a being would be something like a poltergeist or a tinkerbell. The intelligibility of the notion of pure spirit along this route seems to be in direct proportion to its triviality.

Even if such a spirit is conceivable it will not help us in giving content to the notion of a God who is a non-embodied mind. For it was precisely the limitations in space and time that we imagined for such a being which made it possible to individuate it without a body. That is of no assistance towards conceiving of a personal God who is immaterial, ubiquitous and eternal. It is not just that we cannot know what thoughts are God's thoughts, but that there does not seem to be anything which would count as ascribing a thought to God in the way that we can ascribe thoughts to individual human thinkers.

A divine mind would be a mind without a history. In the concept of mind that we apply to human beings, time enters in various ways; but with God there is no variation or shadow of change. God does not change his mind, nor learn, nor forget, nor imagine, nor desire. With us, time enters into both the acquisition and exercise of knowledge, and the onset and satisfaction of wanting. The exercise of knowledge and the execution of desire involves a course of conduct (external or internal) spread over time, which could not be attributed to a being outside time.

The notions of time and change enter into our very concept of intelligence. Intelligence entails speed of acquisition of information, and versatility in adaptation to altered and unforeseen circumstances. In an all-knowing, unchanging being there is no scope for intelligence thus understood. Philosophical understanding is not related to time and change in the same intimate way as is the acquisition and exploitation of information. No doubt this is why, in the tradition going back to Aristotle, it has been taken as a paradigm of divine thought. But the timeless contemplation that Aristotle holds out as the ideal for the philosopher is difficult to make sense of even at the human level.

Reflection on what is involved in the attribution of mentalistic predicates to human beings, and to other finite creatures that resemble them, has brought out for us the enormous difficulty in applying such predicates meaningfully to a being that was infinite and unchanging, and whose field of operation was the entire universe. Philosophy in this area leads to the same conclusion as that of those theologians who have said that when we speak of God we do not know what we are talking about.

6

The Problem of Evil and the Argument from Design

Some 50 years ago the Oxford theologian Austin Farrer published a rich, but since undeservedly neglected, book on rational theology, entitled *Finite and Infinite*.[1] He concluded the book with a section entitled, 'Dialectic of Rational Theology', in which he classified different arguments for the existence of God.

Every argument for God's existence must start from the world of finites: it takes some distinction within the finite, and claims to show that the coexistence of the elements distinguished is intelligible only if God exists as the ground of such a coexistence. Arguments for the existence of God, Farrer maintained, can never be formally valid syllogisms because of the presence of analogical terms (such as 'cause' 'existent') in the

---

[1] Austin Farrer, *Finite and Infinite* (London: Dacre Press, 1943).

premises and the conclusion. But each argument is designed to elicit a cosmological intuition, by presenting a distinction of elements within the creature which makes us jump to the apprehension of God as the being in whom this distinction is transcended.

Arguments for the existence of God will differ from each other according to the finite distinction taken as the basis of each; but they can differ also in the form the argument takes. Let the finite distinction be of the elements A and B. Then we may (1) take A for granted, and show the addition of B to it as necessarily the effect of divine action (or vice versa) or (2) take neither for granted but exhibit the combination AB as forming a nature so 'composite' that it must be regarded as derivative from that which is 'simple' in this respect.

Farrer applies his scheme to a number of familiar and unfamiliar arguments of rational theology – from the distinction essence–existence; from the distinction actual–possible; from the distinction between intellect and will, and so on. I wish to consider here just one of the applications he makes of his scheme: to the argument which he calls the argument 'from Formality and Informality (Chaos)'.

The world, Farrer says, is a composition of form and chaos, each form struggling to dominate the irrelevance of an environment which is chaos relatively to its formal requirements. It is this which is the basis of the argument from design.

In the 1A form, we presuppose chaos. If the world were through and through coherent design, that would be its nature and no explanation would be required.

The mystery is that design should have got such a hold on material lacking form: this must have been imposed from above by a supreme artificer.

> The great difficulty of this argument is the difficulty of presupposing chaos. Chaos is a chaos of forms; stripped of them it is nothing but the spatio-temporal scheme of the interaction of finite forms ... It seems then that we must presuppose not naked chaos, but a chaos of low-grade forms in order to raise the question, how (since these do not need the higher forms for their existence) the higher were imposed upon so recalcitrant a medium. Yet this way of stating the question has its own absurdity; for if, the lowest forms, by themselves formal, can be taken for granted in their chaotic interaction, what fresh principle or fresh difficulty is raised by the interacting of higher forms with one another and with the lower in the same disorder?[2]

Let us change then from the 1A to the 1B pattern, where we presuppose not chaos but forms.

> Surely [form] must have suffered violence from some external power in being thus chaotically interrelated or juxtaposed. This power must himself be supposed exempt from such juxtaposition. If the former argument, presupposing chaos, were absurd in its premise, this argument is absurd in its conclusion. For why should a being, himself completely 'formal', i.e. harmonious, smash finite form against itself in chaotic destruction? The conflict between the argument of the proof and its conclusion is such that it is not usually known as a proof of God, but as the

[2] Ibid., p. 276.

83

'Problem of Evil'. Why should God cause the forms of human and animal existence to break against one another, and against inanimate nature, producing the most appalling deprivations and injuries in the physical sensitive and spiritual orders?[3]

If we advance from pattern 1 to pattern 2, Farrer claims, we both produce an improved version of the argument from design, and we are rid, at a stroke, of the venerable problem of evil. The pattern 2, we remember, is the one which takes neither form nor chaos for granted. Farrer states this version of the argument as follows:

Admitting that the finite, as we know it, is a chaos of forms, we may argue as follows: In so far as there is an element of disorder in the universe, this implies some collocations of substance which cannot be derived from the formal principles of these substances nor from a form of their correlation. Accidental collocation is a mere fact, neither the form nor the expression of any finite operation. It ought to be reduced to a real operation on the part of a being not subject to accidental collocation with other things, nor to the accidental collocation of elements within itself. This non-composite being, then, has placed or created composite being.[4]

Farrer maintains that even thus reformulated, the argument from design, like all arguments for God's existence, involves formal fallacy. None the less, it can, he argues, defy the 'problem of evil' attack:

[3] Ibid.
[4] Ibid.

For granted that existence at our level must be splintered, collocated and accidentally interrelated, it is not a matter of principle just what miseries arise; 'I could believe in God, were it not for cancer' is an absurd contention; for the nature of accident is to be irrational, nor can it be controlled by measure. It is a practical, not a speculative problem: of cancer research, not of theodicy. 'I believe in God because the world is so bad' is as sound an argument as 'I believe in God because the world is so good.' It could not be so bad if it were not so good, since evil is the disease of the good.[5]

Farrer's style is difficult, his terminology often idiosyncratic, and his theory of the relationship between analogical predication and formal fallacy needs careful examination which it will not receive in this essay. None the less, the passages which I have quoted present a number of metaphysical insights which can be detached from their systematic context and restated in terms which many of us may find more familiar. I shall try here to restate and defend the link which Farrer enunciates between the problem of evil and the argument from design: for I believe this to be an insight of fundamental importance in natural theology, and in particular in natural theodicy.

I say 'in *natural* theodicy': because there can be various theodical disciplines, depending on which version of the problem of evil the theologian wishes to dispel. Farrer is concerned, and I shall be concerned, only with the natural problem of evil; and

[5] Ibid., p. 278.

not any of the versions of the supernatural problem of evil.

Let me explain what I mean by this distinction. Let us assume that – as most of the great philosophers throughout history have believed – the world we live in provides us with reason for believing that it is the work of a powerful and good God. Then there is a problem of accounting for the evil it contains; in so far as that can be thought to be traceable to the maker of the world. This is the natural problem of evil which natural theodicy sets out to dispel.

But if we accept that it is possible to know more about God than natural theology provides, then there may be other, perhaps greater, problems of evil. If we believe that God is not just good but positively loves his creatures, then the existence of natural evils becomes that much more difficult to account for. If a revelation claims that God not only permits natural evils but imposes on some of his creatures supernatural evils such as eternal punishment, then the supernatural problem of evil takes a particularly excruciating form. To resolve these problems of evil is a task not for the natural theologian or philosopher of religion, but for the dogmatic theologian, for the professional spokesman for the alleged revelation in question. In this essay I shall restrict myself, as Farrer does in his book, to the natural problem of evil and the province of natural theodicy.

It is a feature which is common to the proof from design and the problem of evil that both are arguments which argue from values to facts. The argument from design can be summarized thus: 'There is a great deal of good in the world: therefore there is a God.' The problem of evil, when used as an argument against theism, proceeds as follows: 'There is a great deal of evil in the world: therefore there is no God.' Those philosophers who are true believers in the logical importance of the fact–value distinction should have no truck with either the proof from design or with the problem of evil. To be sure, it is usually the derivation of values from facts which the fact–value distinction is cried up to exclude. But if values cannot be derived from facts, then facts cannot be derived from values either. Let V be a value-judgement and F a factual statement. If 'If V then F' is a sound principle, then by contraposition so is 'If not F then not V'; hence if a factual statement can be derived from a value-judgement, a value-judgement can be derived from a factual statement. The fact–value barrier must be a two-way barrier, or no barrier at all.

It may have caused surprise, however, that I stated that the argument from design involves value-judgements, at all. Does not the argument from design simply take as its starting point the existence of teleological phenomena in the world? Surely all that teleology involves is a particular pattern of explanation, rather than any reference to good and evil?

Certainly, it was thus that teleological explanation was understood by Descartes, who is commonly awarded the credit, or blame, for cleansing science of teleology. Descartes, it is well-known, rejected the explanation of gravity in terms of attraction between bodies, on the grounds that this postulated in inert bodies knowledge of a goal or terminus. But Descartes was wrong in seeing end-directedness, in this sense, as the distinguishing mark of teleological explanation. The essence of teleological explanation is not the fact that the explanation is given *ex post*, or by reference to the *terminus ad quem*. It is, rather, the part played in the explanation by the notion of purpose: the pursuit of good and the avoidance of evil.

Newtonian inertia and Newtonian gravity provide examples of regularities which are not beneficial for the agents which exhibit them: one is a form of *ex ante* explanation, the other *ex post*. All teleological explanation is in terms of the benefit of agents, but within this there are both *ex ante* regularities (like instinctive avoidance behaviour) and *ex post* regularities (like specific habits of nest-building). Of course there are also teleological explanations of non-regular behaviour, such as human intentional action.

The nature of teleological explanation is often misstated – both by its critics and its defenders. Critics allege that to accept teleology is to accept backwards causation: the production of a cause by its effect. But someone who explains behaviour B of agent A by saying that it is what is required in the circumstances to achieve goal G is not saying that G is the efficient cause of B. On the contrary, B brings G into effect, if it is successful. If B is not successful, G never comes into being; if backwards causation was what was in question we would have here an effect without its cause.

At the other extreme, defenders of teleology have

sometimes claimed that all causation is teleological. Causal laws must be stated in terms of the tendency of causal agents to produce certain effects unless interfered with. But are not laws stated in terms of tendencies teleological laws, since tendencies are defined in terms of their upshot? But an act may be defined by its result, and a tendency specified as a tendency to perform such an act; without the 'end' in the sense of final state being an 'end' in the sense of goal. A tendency is only teleological if it is a tendency to do something for the benefit of the agent, or something bearing a special relation to the agent.

Any teleological explanation must involve an activity which can be done well or badly, or an entity for which there can be good or bad. The paradigm of such entities is the living organism: an entity that has needs, can flourish, can sicken, decay and die. There can be good or bad for things other than whole living organisms: things can be good or bad for the parts, artefacts, environments of living beings. But there are many items – numbers, classes, rocks, dust, mud, elementary particles and the like – for which there is no such thing as good and bad.

Once we have spelt out what is involved in the teleo-logical phenomena which provide the basis for the argument from design, it is clear that the locus of that argument is the same as the locus of the problem of evil. It is the same kind of entity, the same realm of being and the same features of that realm that pro-vide a home for the premisses of both arguments. In order to specify what were the kinds of being to which teleological explanations were appropriate I had to bring in not only the notions of goodness, life and flourishing, but also the notions of badness, decay and death. Whatever can have things good for it can also have things bad for it.

This, as Farrer pointed out, is the first step towards the resolution of the problem of evil. The possibility of goodness brings with it the possibility of badness: if we can describe what is good for X we are *eo ipso* describing that whose lack is bad for X; if in saying that a particular X is a good X we are saying more than simply that it is an X, then there must be the possibility of describing an X which is not a good X. Thus whoever makes a world in which there are things good for things is making a world in which there is the logical possibility of things bad for things.

The problem of evil, of course, is a problem only for those who accept that there is a good creator, or at least a good ruler, of the universe. If the world we see takes its origin and course from iron necessity or blind chance, or some combination of the two, then evil may be regrettable but it is scarcely problematic: what reason have we to expect the world to be anything other than a vale of tears? Not even everyone who accepts the existence of an all-powerful creator need find the existence of evil logically disturbing. The first mover unmoved, the first cause of all, the *ens realissimum*, is not obviously, without considerable further argument, a source of goodness. It is the argument from design which leads to the conclusion that there is an extramundane origin precisely for purpose and the pursuit of good.

Consideration of the argument from design, therefore, is related to the resolution of the problem of evil in two different ways. If one rejects the argument, then one is, so far as natural theology is concerned, freed from the logical constraints of the problem of evil. If one accepts the argument, then one accepts along with it at least a partial recipe for the problem's solution: for the author of goodness to which the argument leads is by logical necessity the author of the possibility of evil.

This goes part of the way to the problem's solution: but must we not go much further? Must the logical possibility be actualized in the real world? Could not omnipotence make a world in which the possibility remained no more than a possibility?

The world we live in seems to have two features – emphasized by Farrer – which go beyond the necessity imposed by the nature of good and evil. In the first place, it is a world in which form survives by the precarious management of chaos: in which, for instance, my intellectual and animal life organizes the chemical and physical material in which it is embodied. Secondly, it is a world in which the organisms of various forms compete with each other for the matter to be organized: in which predators live off their prey and there is competition not only between but within species for the benefits offered by the environment.

A material world of precarious competition is the only world of which we have experience, and our imaginations are too feeble for us to be sure whether other forms of world are genuinely conceivable. The most sustained effort to imagine beings whose forms were not enthroned on chaos was the angelology of the medieval scholastics. It is difficult to be confident whether the immaterial spirits of scholastic tradition are genuinely conceivable or not; it is even more difficult to have much hope that we shall do better than the scholastics in this area in drawing limits to conceivability which are firm enough to rest an argument upon. We may, I think, accept with Farrer that a world containing any beings whom we could conceive of as having good would also have the actuality, and not just the possibility, of evil, because of the interlocking of one creature's good with another's evil. This is something which we must accept; as he puts it: 'As we love our own distinct being, so must we endure the conditions of its possibility.'[6]

Suppose we accept, then, that any world containing good must contain the possibility of evil, and also that any world of the kind that has the likes of us in it must have the actuality of evil. Can one not still maintain that only a brute or blackguard would create the world we actually have? To consider this we have to take a further step in the consideration both of the problem of evil and of the argument from design.

Why is the presence of good and evil in the world supposed to call for an extraterrestrial source? We don't, after all, think that the presence of hot and cold in the world means that there has to be an extra-terrestrial fount of heat: what is special about good and evil?

The argument from design turns on the fact that much of the good which is present in the world is present in the form of purpose. (I put on one side the question whether there could be a world in which there was good but only accidental good; whether or not such a world is possible, ours is not such a world.) There are things which exist to serve purposes (e.g. organs with their distinct functions) and there are things which have purposes (e.g. animals with their characteristic activities).

I must avert a misunderstanding here: having a purpose does not involve, necessarily, knowledge or intention of that purpose. Not all purposes of entities are conscious goals or projects of that entity. The activity of the spider has as its purpose the construction of the web, as the activity of the dog has as its purpose the retrieval of a bone; but the dog is conscious of the purpose as the spider is not. Not all purposeful actions are intentional actions, and not all entities with purposes are entities that have been designed by those whose needs they serve. Whether or not my liver was designed by God, it was not designed by me.

'Purpose', then, does not mean the same as 'design'. The argument from design aims to show that all purpose originates from design – but it does not assume this as if it was a tautology. Design is purpose which derives from a conception of the good which fulfils the purpose. If the conclusion of the argument from design is correct, then all purpose is of this kind. But that is not something to be assumed at the outset.

Nowadays, however, both proponents and critics of the argument from design accept the premiss that naked purpose is inconceivable. That is to say, if we have an explanation in terms of purpose, that cannot be a fundamental, rock-bottom explanation. The explanation must be reducible to an explanation in terms of design, that is to say intelligent purpose; or to explanation of a mechanistic kind, in terms of necessity, chance, or both. Theists opt for the first kind of explanation, many evolutionary biologists for the second.

There are five levels at which prima facie there is purpose operative in the universe: first, the operation of mature living organisms; second, the operation of organs within those organisms; third, the morphogenesis of the individual from the embryonic state; fourth, the emergence of new species; fifth, the origin of speciation and of life itself. At each of these levels purpose may seem to call for a designer; at each level one who wishes to resist this conclusion must reduce the teleological elements to mechanistic ones, claiming to show how the evolution of life is either an inevitable process, explained by the natural properties of non-living matter, or the result of the operation of necessitating forces upon the outcome of chance occurrences.

I shall not consider in detail the plausibility or otherwise of mechanistic reduction of teleology, at each of these five levels. I shall assume, for the sake of argument, that at one or other point the reduction breaks down, so that the argument from design succeeds. I ask what consequences follow for the problem of evil and the responsibility of the cosmic designer?

The answer seems to differ according to the method by which the design operates or, if you like, the point or points at which the purposiveness is introduced from outside into the cosmic story. The first case, and the easiest one to judge, is the one in which the designer achieves his purpose, and the purposes of his creatures, by the operation of necessitating laws. In such a world, it seems, God would be not only the author of evil, but the author of sin. As I put it in *The God of the Philosophers*:

> If an agent freely and knowingly sets in motion a deterministic process with a certain upshot, it seems that he must be responsible for that upshot. Calvin argued rightly that the truth of determinism would not make everything that happens in the world happen by God's intention: only some of the events of history would be chosen by God as ends or means, others could be merely consequences of his choices. But that would not suffice to acquit God of responsibility for sin. For moral agents are responsible not only for their intentional actions; but also for the consequences of their actions: for states of affairs which they bring about voluntarily but not intentionally. An indeterminist can make a distinction between those states of affairs which God causes, and those which he merely permits: but in a deterministic created universe, the distinction between causing and permitting would have no application to God.[7]

[7] Anthony Kenny, *The God of the Philosophers* (Oxford: Oxford University Press, 1979), p. 86.

This consideration is unlikely greatly to trouble a proponent of the argument from design, since our universe does not appear to be one in which determinism reigns, but rather one in which, while there are effects which are determined by causes, there are also events which are determined only by coming to pass. Indeed, the mechanistic opponents of the argument from design themselves commonly seek to reduce purpose not to determinist necessity but to the operation of necessity upon chance events.

We must look more closely at what we mean by chance, considered as an explanatory factor. One is the chance which is the unsought outcome of the operation of one or more causes (where more than one cause is in play this kind of chance is coincidence). The other kind of chance is the tendency to produce its proper effect n times out of m. The two kinds may be linked together in a particular case: a throw of a double six when dicing is an instance of both kinds of chance. Chance in the second sense is a genuine – if indeterministic – principle of explanation.

Freedom is not the same thing as chance. An action is free if it is the exercise of a voluntary power. A voluntary power differs from a natural power in being a two-way power. The notion of chance applies to voluntary powers no less than to natural powers. Just as one kind of chance consists in the coincidental exercise of the natural powers of unrelated agents, so another kind of chance consists in the coincidental operation of non-conspiring voluntary causes.

It is often claimed that allowing the reality of freedom and chance in our world is the key to resolving the
problem of evil. This, I believe, is not so.

First, if compatibilism is true, as I have argued on
several occasions elsewhere, then the acknowledgement
of freedom does not even rule out the possibility
of the deterministic universe in which God would
undoubtedly be the author of sin.

Secondly, the kinds of chance we have recognized
are compatible both with design and with the responsibility of the designer. A designer may put together two
non-conspiring causes in such a way that the outcome
is one not sought (pursued, tended towards) by either
cause; he may include among the causes the indeterministic ones (as a computer-programmer may include
a randomizing element in his program). In neither case
would he avoid responsibility for what happens, despite
the attempt by Descartes to show the contrary in
his celebrated parable of the king who both forbids
duelling but brings two inveterate duellers together in a
quarrel.

What of undesigned chance: will that absolve
the maker of the world for responsibility for the evils
it contains? Evils which are the consequences of
undesigned chance would be neither means nor
ends of the Great Designer. They would be risks
which he takes knowingly, in general, of the nature
of the risk, but without knowledge, in particular,
of the evils which will in fact eventuate. A designer
who takes risks of this kind would be less, I
have argued elsewhere, than the God of traditional

Western theism, because he would not have full knowledge of the future. But our present question is: would he avoid responsibility for the evils of the world?

The natural response is to say that it all depends whether the game is worth the candle: whether the goods to be achieved are worth the risk of the evil. If this is so, then only a global view of the totality of good and evil to be found in the achieved universe would enable one to cast the accounts. And this means that no impugner of divine goodness could hope to make his prosecution succeed: for the evidence which could alone secure a conviction is available only to the accused, and not even to him in advance of the end of the cosmic drama.

Note that a theist could adopt this response to the problem of evil without taking the view that no moral judgement is possible about God. For if he is, as he is likely to be, an absolutist in morals, he will agree that there are certain things God could not do and remain good: such as telling lies, or punishing the innocent everlastingly. He will not need to adopt the consequentialist view that moral judgement on an action – whether a human action or a divine action – must wait on a full conspectus of the consequences. It is only in the case where evil is risked – not when it is knowingly permitted or wilfully brought about – that the felicific calculus is allowed to have moral weight.

But this kind of reflection brings about the unreality of the exercise we have been engaged in. It must be doubtful whether cosmic judgements of the form 'the world is on balance a good/bad place' have any clear sense; anyone who believes they have must believe that the sense of a judgement is totally divorced from the possibility of the judge's putting himself into a position to have adequate grounds for the judgement. It is hard enough to attach sense to much more modest generalizations such as 'The human race is on the whole a good/bad thing' or 'People in the twentieth century are happier/unhappier than people were in the twelfth century.'

If it is difficult to attach clear sense to the evidence to be brought against the designer of the world, it is even more difficult to take seriously the idea of calling him before the bar of human morality. Morality presupposes a moral community, and a moral community must be of beings with a common language, roughly equal powers and roughly similar needs, desires and interests. God can no more be part of a moral community with human beings than he can be part of a political community with them. As Aristotle said, we cannot attribute moral virtues to divinity: the praise would be vulgar. Equally, moral blame would be laughable.

Remember that we have been speaking throughout within the bounds of natural theology. If an alleged revelation claims that God has entered into moral relationships with human beings, then we enter into a different realm of discourse; but if that discourse can be made intelligible, the present difficulty is one that will have to be surmounted along with others. Within the realm of a purely natural theology there is no problem of evil, but equally we must retract the claim that the argument from design showed God to be good.

Farrer was right to say that 'I believe in God because the world is so bad' is as sound an argument as 'I believe in God because the world is so good.' But he did not follow sufficiently rigorously his own insight that the arguments for the existence of God start from a division within the finite and show that that insight is transcended in the infinite. Farrer was right to show that the argument from design and the problem of evil are two formulations of a single progress from the finite dichotomy of good and evil to an infinite in which that dichotomy is transcended. But that progress leads to a God which is no more the source of good than the source of evil. The God to which this argument of rational theology leads is not supreme goodness: it is a being which is beyond good and evil.

7

Faith, Pride and Humility

Among the traits which our religious tradition holds up as virtues there are two that are especially Christian: one is faith and the other is humility. It is not that these, according to Christian teaching, are the greatest virtues: it is charity that is above all. But charity, in itself, is not something upheld as a virtue only by Christianity: the great commandment to love God and one's neighbour is, after all, an Old Testament command recalled in the New. What makes the contrast between Judaism and Christianity is above all the role Christianity assigns to faith. Faith in the broad sense of trust in God is to be found, as Paul insisted, in the heroes of the Old Testament from Abraham onwards. But faith in the stricter sense of adherence to religious doctrine is something to which Christianity assigns a novel role. It is only in Christianity that the reciting of a creed is the hallmark of adherence to a religion. Even the nature of charity is affected by this change. In classical Christian theology it is impossible truly to love God and man unless one's charity is based on true faith.

If it is the role of faith which contrasts Christianity with Judaism, it is humility whose role marks out Christianity from paganism, ancient and modern. The good man as described in Aristotle's *Nicomachean Ethics* is not humble: he is great-souled, that is to say he is a highly superior being who is well aware of his own superiority to others. In our own age we insist on individual rights: systematic attempts are made to raise people's consciousness of their rights and to urge them to insist on exacting them. All this creates a climate in which humility appears a highly suspect virtue.

Within Christianity itself, I shall maintain, there is a tension between the two attitudes: that of humility and that of faith. Indeed, I shall claim that humility, rightly understood, is incompatible with faith, as traditionally understood. Faith and humility, I shall argue, cannot both be genuine virtues. If we must choose, then our choice should favour the claims of humility rather than those of dogmatic faith.

For there is no doubt that humility is a virtue, and a precious one. But its merits need defence, for there were and are those who consider it no virtue. First of all, in one's own case, is it not a lapse from truthfulness to judge oneself worse than one deserves? Secondly, in the case of others, is there not something odious in the preaching of humility by persons in positions of power and privilege to others less favoured than themselves? When the poor and weak are contented with their lowly station, it is the rich and powerful who stand to gain. These objections to humility need to be taken seriously; yet humility rightly understood is a virtue of great price.

True humility, however, needs to be distinguished from specious and irrelevant forms of humility. There is an obvious and irritating counterfeit of humility that finds expression in insincere utterances of self-abasement. This was the humility that was parodied by Charles Dickens in the character of Uriah Heep; but already Augustine had denounced it, saying that feigned humility, which is expressed only in exterior gestures, is the greatest of pride.[1]

But there are more respectable kinds of humility which do not yet reach the heart of the matter. There is the tactical humility that finds expression in a modest and unassuming approach. If I decide I have a duty to rebuke a colleague, there is more likelihood of success if I begin the conversation not with 'I think you have behaved disgracefully', but with 'There is a matter on which I would value your advice.' This tactical humility is not real humility: it is not based on any judgement that my interlocutor is, in the relevant respect, my superior. It is not, however, a vice: it is a harmless necessary managerial skill. It would seem vulgar to regard it as any kind of virtue had it not been commended to us by Jesus himself in the context of seating-plans at table.

There is another kind of humility, insisted on in

[1] IIa IIae, 1 ad 2.

Christian tradition, which might be called metaphysical humility. This is the humility of an individual before God, based on the reflection that in comparison with God any creature is dust, ashes and nothingness. The problem about metaphysical humility is that it has little relevance to any moral virtue governing relations between human beings. If I am dust, ashes and nothingness, so are you; at the level of dust that need not prevent me thinking that I am ever so superior to you. In the light of eternity no doubt differences of worth between us are insignificant, but in the bustle of workaday life and in the competition for transitory goods and honours one can cancel out the meta-physical humility as a common denominator under-lying all human value and excellence.

The real humility is the one that is expressed in a text of St Paul: 'In lowliness of mind let each esteem other better than themselves' (Phil. 2, 3). How can this be possible, one may wonder; and, if possible, how can it be a virtue? St Thomas Aquinas, having insisted that true humility involves the subjection of a human being in the face of God,[2] goes on to say, with his robust good sense, that it cannot be a virtue to believe oneself the worst of all sinners. If we all did that, then all but one of us would be believing a falsehood, and it cannot be the part of virtue to promote false belief. St Thomas glosses the text as follows. What is good in each of us comes from God; all we can really call our own is our

[2] IIa IIae, 161, 2 ad 3; 3,1.

sinfulness. Every one, with respect to what is his own, should regard himself as less than his neighbour in respect of what there is of God in his neighbour. But, he goes on to say, 'Humility does not require that someone should regard less the gifts of God in himself than the gifts of God in others.' But whatever gifts an individual has received from God, he can always find gifts that others have received and he has not; and when comparing himself with others those are the matters on which he should fix his mind.[3]

This is no doubt sound advice; and yet I do not feel that St Thomas's account of the virtue is adequate. He does not explain how humility can involve placing others above oneself, and yet not deviate from a just appreciation of one's gifts. He defines humility as the virtue that restrains the appetite from pursuing great things beyond reason.[4] It is the virtue that is the moderation of ambition – not its contradiction but its moderation. It is based on, though not identical with, a just appreciation of one's own defects. By an astonishing piece of intellectual legerdemain St Thomas makes it not only compatible with but a counterpart of the alleged Aristotelian virtue of magnanimity. Humility, he says, ensures that one's ambitions are based on a just assessment of one's defects, magnanimity that they are based on a just assessment of one's gifts.[5]

To me it seems that Christian humility demands, and

[3] Ibid., IIa IIae 161, 3c.
[4] Ibid., IIa IIae 161, 1c.
[5] Ibid., IIa IIae 161 1, ad3.

rightly, more than a just assessment of one's own defects. Humility is a virtue which concerns one's assessment of one's own merits and defects in comparison with others. The virtues, as Aristotle taught us, concern particular passions; they assist reason to control these passions. The relevant passion in this quarter is the raging tempest of self-love: our inclination to overvalue our own gifts, overesteem our own opinions and place excessive importance on getting our own way. Humility is the virtue that counteracts this prejudice. It does so not by making the *judgement* that one's own gifts are lesser than others, or that one's own opinions are falser than others – for that, as St Thomas says, would often lead to falsehood. It does so, rather, by making the *presumption* that others' talents are greater, others' opinions more likely to be right. Like all presumptions, the presumption of humility is rebuttable; it may be that for a particular purpose one's own gifts are more adapted than those of one's neighbours; on a particular topic it may be that one is right and one's neighbour wrong. But only by approaching each conflict of interest and opinion with this presumption can one hope to escape the myopia that magnifies everything to do with oneself by comparison with everything to do with others.

Humility is itself a humble virtue. It is easy enough to see the ugliness of the contrary vice of pride. Every day we notice people defending theses that are indefensible, taking on jobs they are unsuited for, taking offence at imagined slights. But if a person has humility, it often takes an effort for others to realize this. It takes observation to notice that it is so-and-so who always takes the lowest jobs; that whoever is thrusting into the limelight, it is not her but someone else. Not that humility necessarily means an avoidance of the public eye; it takes a certain humility to be willing to stick one's neck out and place oneself in a position to make a public fool of oneself.

Humility, thus understood, can be seen to be a moral virtue without any appeal to Christian doctrine or to specifically religious premises. None the less, it is one of the great gifts of Christianity to the human race to have identified and exalted this virtue. It has done so by presenting heroes and patterns of imitation who were humbly placed and degraded in the eyes of the world: a crucified son and a mother whose only extant work is a hymn to the Lord who put down the mighty and exalted the lowly. Even the pride of Christians expressed itself in the language of humility: so that if a man claimed to be the spiritual lord of Christendom, he gave himself the title 'servant of the servants of God'.

As befits a Christian saint, Aquinas himself displays great humility in his writings. If anything he is too willing to defer to the opinions of others, too ready to interpret benignly the writings of his predecessors. As has been said, he was unable to make a wholly convincing attempt to reconcile Aristotle's teaching on magnanimity with Christian preaching of humility. None the less, we can recognize not only in Aquinas but also in Aristotle himself the virtue which it took Christianity to canonize. Among all the philosophers who, throughout the ages, have displayed genius of the first rank, the two whose works display least attachment to their own ego are Aristotle and Aquinas.

While praising the characteristic Christian virtue of humility, I have expressed reservation about the other Christian attribute of faith. The recitation of a creed, I claim, is incompatible with the true humility which Christianity so rightly prizes. This may seem surprising, as faith is so often held up as an exercise of humility: the abasement of the human reason before the mysterious power of God. Now of course if God has indeed revealed some truths, it would be insane folly not to accept them. The difficulty is in knowing first that there is a God; and secondly that he has revealed certain doctrines. For my part I find the arguments for God's existence unconvincing and the historical evidence uncertain on which the credal statements are based. The appropriate response to the uncertainty of argument and evidence is not atheism – that is at least as rash as the theism to which it is opposed – but agnosticism: that is the admission that one does not know whether there is a God who has revealed himself to the world.

There is, beyond doubt, a virtue – let us call it rationality – which preserves the just mean between believing too much (credulity) and believing too little (scepticism). From the viewpoint of an agnostic both the theist and the atheist err by credulity: they are both believing something – the one a positive proposition, the other a negative proposition – in the absence of the appropriate justification. On the other hand, from the point of view of theism, the agnostic errs on the side of scepticism: that is, he has no view on a topic on which it is very important to have a view. Internally, there is no way of settling whether it is the agnostic who errs on the side of scepticism, or the theist who is erring on the side of credulity.

But if we look at the matter from the viewpoint of humility it seems that the agnostic is in the safer position. The general presumption that others are in the right will not help us here; for others are to be found in both camps, and there is no obvious way to decide to which of them one should bow. But there is one important difference. The theist is claiming to possess a good which the agnostic does not claim to possess: he is claiming to be in possession of knowledge; the agnostic lays claim only to ignorance. The believer will say he does not claim knowledge, only true belief; but at least he claims to have laid hold, in whatever way, of information that the agnostic does not possess. It may be said that any claim to possess gifts which others do not have is in the same situation, and yet we have admitted that such a claim may be made with truth and without prejudice to humility. But in the case of a gift such as intelligence or athletic skill, those surpassed will agree that they are surpassed; whereas in this case, the theist can only rely on the support of other theists, and the agnostic does not think that the information which the theist claims is genuine information at all. Since Socrates philosophers have realized that a claim not to know is easier to support than a claim to know.

8

Two Agnostic Poets: Arthur Hugh Clough and Matthew Arnold

Arthur Hugh Clough and Matthew Arnold had over-lapping careers at Oxford between 1838 and 1849. Both of them came to Balliol from Rugby School as devout members of the Church of England; both of them, before they left Oxford, had lost their Anglican faith. Both of them became, in effect, agnostics; and both in their poetry have left evidence of the melancholy aspects of Victorian agnosticism – of which Arnold's 'Dover Beach' is the best-known and Clough's 'Easter Day' the most eloquent. But we must remember that for the young Arnold, and for the young Clough loss of faith was initially a liberation.

First, it was an intellectual liberation – it was seizing the chance to disbelieve in parts of Christian tradition that they believed, rightly or wrongly, the progress of science and criticism had shown to be untenable. It was claiming the right to believe there were errors in the Bible, and the right to disbelieve in the metaphysics of natural theology. Above all, it was claiming the right to believe that there was salvation outside the Christian Church.

For Clough, subscription to the Thirty-Nine Articles of the Church of England was a fetter on intellectual enquiry which had to be thrown off. For his friend Arthur Stanley, still a believer, but who refused to be ordained until he was assured he need not believe in the damnatory clauses of the Athanasian Creed, subscription could be a violation of charity. For all Victorians, the overthrow of traditional Church doctrine – whether the doctrine of the high and dry Anglicans or of the Romeward-leaning Tractarians – was a liberation from fear.

Matthew Arnold has sometimes been criticized for a facile belief in progress and a failure to foresee future catastrophes such as the Holocaust. It is true that Arnold's melancholy about the present was sometimes balanced by an exaggerated optimism about the future. But neither he, nor any of his generation, can be accused of never having faced the possibility that the human condition is irredeemably evil. The holocaust that the Athanasian creed threatened to all but a tiny minority of the human race was a holocaust in comparison with which Auschwitz was humane. It was torture by burning, not gassing; it was pain that was eternal and not momentary.

Clough, when he wrote in January 1848 to give Matthew Arnold's brother Tom the news of his resignation of his tutorship, wrote as follows: 'I feel greatly rejoiced to think that this is my last term of bondage in Egypt, though I shall, I suppose, quit the fleshpots for a wilderness, with small hope of manna, quails, or water from the rock.' Many Christians, however, overthrew belief in Hell without becoming agnostic. How many nowadays who describe themselves as Christians and worship in Christian churches believe in the literal truth of an everlasting Hell? Yet few think of themselves as agnostics.

Agnosticism is a stance taken in relation to God rather than in relation to Christianity. Some who gave up all Christian belief came to disbelieve in God and became atheists. Arnold was repelled by the belligerent atheism of Bradlaugh, as many non-Christians of a later age have been repelled by that of Ayer and Dawkins. Arnold decided that he could continue to describe himself as a Christian; but he was only a Christian in the sense in which a philosopher can be a Platonist or a Wittgensteinian. He was not a serious theist, and is best described as agnostic.

In *Literature and Dogma* Arnold speaks of God as an 'eternal power, not ourselves, that makes for righteousness'.[1] Elsewhere he speaks of God as 'the stream of tendency by which all things seek to fulfil the law of their being'.[2] His attempts at a literal description of

---

[1] Matthew Arnold, *Literature and Dogma*, in *The Complete Prose Works of Matthew Arnold*, Vol. 6, ed. R. H. Super (Ann Arbor, MI: University of Michigan Press, 1965), p. 340.

[2] Ibid., p. 344.

God are all similarly disastrous, provoking hilarity among both believers and unbelievers.

Arnold was better inspired when he said that the language of the Bible is literary not scientific language; language thrown out as an object of consciousness, or fully grasped, that inspired emotion. 'God' is one of the literary terms that cannot be used scientifically. The real object of religion is conduct, which is three-quarters of life. Proofs of religious doctrine from prophecy and miracle are not to his taste. 'There is nothing one would more desire for a person or document one greatly values, than to make them independent of miracles.'[3]

Arnold rejected not only Christian dogma but also belief in an afterlife. The philosophical arguments for immortality have no substance. The typical idea of heaven, Arnold said, is of a perfected middle-class home, with labour ended, the table spread, goodness all around, the lost ones restored, hymnody incessant. 'That this conception of immortality cannot possibly be true, we feel, the moment we conceive it clearly. And yet who can devise any conception of a future state of being, which shall bear close examination better?'[4]

In a later work, A Psychological Parallel,[5] Arnold insists that his wish is to assert the truth and importance of Christianity against those who disparaged

[3] Ibid., p. 183.
[4] Ibid., p. 166.
[5] Matthew Arnold, A Psychological Parallel, ibid., p. 364.

them. But he agrees that it is hard to think of a man taking orders in the Church of England who accepted the view of Christianity offered in *Literature and Dogma*. For the Church of England presents as science, and as necessary to salvation, what it is the very object of that book to show to be not science and not necessary to salvation. A layman in the Church does not have to use the Articles. But he has to rehearse the prayers and services of the Church.

> Much of these he may rehearse as the literal, beautiful rendering of what he himself feels and believes. The rest he may rehearse as an approximate rendering of it – as language thrown out by other men, at other times, at immense objects which deeply engage their affections and awe, and which deeply engage his also; objects concerning which, moreover, adequate statement is impossible. To him, therefore, this approximate part of the prayers and service which he rehearses will be poetry.[6]

It is a great error, Arnold says in conclusion, to think that whatever is perceived to be poetry ceases to be available to religion. The noblest races are those that know how to make the most serious use of poetry.

However unconvincing some of Arnold's revisions of Christianity may appear, they are at some distance from the utter void of faith suggested by 'Dover Beach', the best known of his poems and the classic statement of the Victorian crisis of belief.

[6] Ibid., p. 236.

Describing the ebb and flow of the tide in the English Channel (and, rather less plausibly, in the Aegean) Arnold says:

> The Sea of Faith
> Was once, too, at the full, and round earth's shore
> Lay like the folds of a bright girdle furl'd
> But now I only hear
> Its melancholy, long, withdrawing roar,
> Retreating, to the breath
> Of the night-wind, down the vast edges drear
> And naked shingles of the world.

The believer, once buoyed up by the full tide of faith, can now, in an age of scepticism, only stub his bare toes on the dry hard pebbles of scientific fact.

'Dover Beach' is widely believed to have been written on Arnold's honeymoon. But already another honeymoon poem strikes a different note. In 'Stanzas from the Grande Chartreuse', on the way to answering the question, 'What am I, that I am here?' (namely, in the monastery), Arnold tells us that 'rigorous teachers seized my youth / And purg'd its faith and trimm'd its fire'. In visiting the Chartreuse, he insists, he is not denying the lessons he learned from those teachers. Rather he compares himself to a Greek looking at prehistoric Nordic ruins; a Greek, perhaps like the Sophocles of 'Dover Beach' who compared the tide to the ebb and flow of human misery.

'Both were faiths, and both were gone', Arnold says. The two departed faiths are presumably two out of the three: Catholic monasticism, ancient Olympus, Nordic ruins. Which two is not, to me at least, totally clear. But the important thing is that Arnold is waiting for a new world to be born. It may be that a new faith is to be born – as one was born after Sophocles. The tide retreating with its melancholy long withdrawing roar may yet come in again. 'Dover Beach' itself could well have ended differently; the final despairing verse of the poem is separable from the stanza on the outgoing tide.

Among the rigorous teachers who purged Arnold's faith an important one, I suggest, was Arthur Hugh Clough himself. We may note first, that Clough was, literally, Arnold's tutor, and was responsible for his obtaining a respectable degree. But more importantly, the ideas of Clough in the 1840s were the same as those of Arnold in the 1850s.

The discrediting of dogma is nowhere expressed with greater force and firmness than in Clough's poem 'Easter Day', written in 1849, but published only posthumously:

> Christ is not risen, no
> He lies and moulders low
> Christ is not risen.
>
> Ashes to ashes, dust to dust
> As of the unjust also of the just
> Christ is not risen.
>
> Ye hills, fall on us, and ye mountains cover!
>   In darkness and great gloom
> Come ere we thought it is our day of doom,
> From the cursed world which is one tomb
>   Christ is not risen.

Eat, drink, and die, for we are men deceived,
Of all the creatures under heaven's wide cope
We are most hopeless who had once most hope
We are most wretched that had most believed
    Christ is not risen.

But Clough, while thus dramatizing disbelief, was not at all certain that the critical and scientific scepticism of the age was the last word on the future of religion. See what he says in 'The New Sinai', a poem that Arnold praised, rather condescendingly, when it was first published in 1849:

God spake it out, 'I, God, am One';
    The unheeding ages ran
And baby-thoughts again, again
    Have dogged the growing man;
And as of old from Sinai's top
    God said that God is One,
By Science strict so speaks He now
    To tell us, There is None!
Earth goes by chemic forces; Heaven's
    A Mecanique Celeste
And heart and mind of human kind
    A watch-work as the rest!

Is this a Voice, as was the Voice
    Whose speaking told abroad,
When thunder pealed and mountain reeled
    The ancient truth of God?
Ah, not the Voice; 'tis but the cloud
    The outer darkness dense,
Where image none, nor e'er was seen
    Similitude of sense.

> 'Tis but the cloudy darkness dense
>   That wrapt the Mount around;
> When in amaze the people stays
>   To hear the Coming Sound.
>
> . . .
>
> 'Tis but the cloudy darkness dense
>   Though blank the tale it tells
> No God, no Truth! Yet He, in sooth,
>   Is there – within it dwells;
> Within the sceptic darkness deep
>   He dwells that none may see,
> Till idol forms and idol thoughts
>   Have passed and cease to be.

The moral was that one should neither relapse, like the Puseyites, into the infantile idolatry of the Golden Calf, nor accept the current atheism of science as the last word from the mystic mountain. Mankind should neither reject science, nor embrace superstition, but wait in faith for God to complete his plan of revelation.

Arnold and Clough were very close in the early 1840s – the years of the excursions to Thames-side villages described in Arnold's 'Thyrsis' and 'Scholar-Gipsy'. We know from the reminiscences of Thomas Arnold that these continued over the years to come. From Clough's diaries we can tell that Arnold's companionship brought to an end a long period of tortured moral introspection: it showed him the possibility of friendship without guilt, and the way to relate to pupils without embarrassment. Arnold also gave Clough the power to resist the overwhelming charisma of

Newman, while the three of them were Oriel colleagues together.

If that is what Arnold gave to Clough, what did Clough give to Arnold? Because Arnold has a greater repute as a poet and critic, because Arnold outlived Clough and had the last word on their relationship, it is easy to forget that Clough was the senior of the two, and had a significant hand in the formation of his character. Arnold in old age gained the reputation of a solemn sage; as an undergraduate his reputation was that of an idle dandy.

In 'Thyrsis', the monody Arnold published in commemoration of Clough's death, he compares his friend's search for the truth with that of the scholar-gypsy of his earlier poem.

Thou, too, O Thyrsis, on like quest wert bound,
Thou wanderedst with me for a little hour.
   Men gave thee nothing; but this happy quest,
If men esteem'd thee feeble, gave thee power,
If men procured thee trouble, gave thee rest.
   And this rude Cumner ground,
Its fir-topped Hurst, its farms, its quiet fields,
   Here cam'st thou in thy jocund youthful time,
   Here was thine height of strength, thy golden prime!
And still the haunt beloved a virtue yields.

What though the music of thy rustic flute
Kept not for long its happy country tone;
   Lost it too soon, and learnt a stormy note
Of men contention-tost, of men who groan
   Which task'd thy pipe too sore, and tired thy throat—
   It fail'd, and thou wert mute.

This stanza seems to be a plain reversal of the truth in its suggestion that Clough's talent declined after the years of their Oxford companionship. The verse that Clough wrote in Oxford, while it contained some powerful pieces, was in general mediocre, often religiously lachrymose and almost uniformly sombre. It was after he broke with the Church of England and left Oxford in 1848 that he wrote all his best poems. The two most powerful and polished – 'The Bothie of Tober-na-Vuolich' and 'Amours de Voyage' – belong to the years that followed his departure. These began with the year of the revolutions in Europe's capitals, revolutions of which Clough was a spectator, first in Paris between the fall of Louis-Philippe and the coup of Napoleon III, then in Rome during Garibaldi's defence of the Roman Republic against the Pope's French allies. Those years were Clough's prime and liberation, not the years in Oxford, even the happiest best years that he shared with Arnold.

In the 1840s Arnold and Clough conducted poetic dialogues with each other. In 1848 Arnold wrote two sonnets 'to a Republican Friend'. His long poem 'Resignation to Fausta', a solemn work of rural mountainous elevation, drew a jaunty response from Clough, 'Resignation to Faustus', which sets out an urban reconciliation between the sublime and the sordid in our life. But most important, for our purpose, is Clough's repeated return to the themes of 'Dover Beach'.

In Clough's dramatic drama 'Dipsychus', a dialogue

between a hesitant Faust-like figure and a buoyant Mephistopheles-like spirit, the protagonist has a dream:

> I dreamt a dream; till morning light
> A bell rang in my head all night
> Tinkling and tinkling first, and then
> Tolling; and tinkling; tolling again.
> So brisk and gay, and then so slow!
> O joy, and terror! mirth, and woe!
> Ting-ting, there is no God, dong,
> There is no God; dong, dong!
>
> Ting-ting, there is no God; ting-ting;
> Come dance and play, and merrily sing –
> Ting, ting-a-ding; ting, ting-a-ding
> O pretty girl who trippest along
> Come to my bed – it isn't wrong.
> Uncork the bottle, sing the song!
> Ting, ting-a-ding; dong, dong.
> Wine has dregs, the song an end
> A silly girl is a poor friend
> And age and weakness who shall mend?
> Dong, there is no God; Dong.

These first two of nine stanzas set the tone for the whole. In each stanza the first half sets out the joyful and mirthful consequences of the hypothesis that there is no God, while the second portrays its consequences of woe and terror. The bell first tinkles out the liberating aspects of atheism, and then tolls out its doleful consequences. The fourth stanza, for instance, concerns the life of love:

> O Rosalie, my precious maid,
> I think thou thinkest love is true;
> And on thy fragrant bosom laid
> I almost could believe it too.
> O, in our nook, unknown, unseen,
> We'll hold our fancy like a screen
> Us and the dreadful fact between.
> And it shall yet be long, aye long,
> The quiet notes of our low song
> Shall keep us from that sad dong, dong.
> Hark, hark, hark! O voice of fear!
> It reaches us here, even here!
> Dong, there is no God; dong.

Dipsychus' dream recalls the sombre mood of the final stanza of 'Dover Beach' where Arnold, in a world devoid of faith, offers human love as the only consolation:

> Ah, love, let us be true
> To one another! For the world, which seems
> To lie before us like a land of dreams,
> So various, so beautiful, so new,
> Hath really neither joy, nor love, nor light
> Nor certitude, nor peace, nor help for pain . . .

The address to the beloved surely offers only inconsistent consolation: if there is no love and no certitude in the real world, how can one rely on the truth of the beloved? Clough's final stanza rejects this inconsistency:

> But Rosalie, my lovely maid,
> I think thou thinkest love is true;

And on thy faithful bosom laid
I almost could believe it too.
The villainies, the wrongs, the alarms
Forget we in each other's arms
No justice here, no God above;
But where we are, is there not love?
What? What? thou also go'st? For how
Should dead truth live in lover's vow?
What thou? Thou also lost? Dong
Dong, there is no God; dong!

Dipsychus' dream is more consistent than Arnold's poem. But Arnold's pessimism is more complete than Clough's. For Arnold it is the beauty of the world that is the dream; for Clough it is the sombre tolling of the bell of atheism. Clough's poem ends with the dreamer waking, and this withdrawal from the brink of despair weakens the poem aesthetically, making its end mawkish and anticlimactic.

Clough's last word on the question of God's existence is more light-hearted and aesthetically more successful:

'There is no God' the wicked saith,
  'and truly it's a blessing
For what he might have done with us
  It's better only guessing.'

'There is no God' a youngster thinks,
  'Or really, if there may be
He surely didn't mean a man
  Always to be a baby.'

THE UNKNOWN GOD

'There is no God, or if there is'
  The tradesman thinks, ''Twere funny
If he should take it ill in me
  To make a little money.'

'Whether there be' the rich man says,
  'It matters very little,
For I and mine, thank somebody
  Are not in want of victual.'

Some others, also, to themselves
  Who scarce so much as doubt it,
Think there is none, when they are well,
  And do not think about it.

But country folks who live beneath
  The shadow of the steeple
The parson and the parson's wife
  And mostly married people

Youths green and happy in first love,
  So thankful for illusion;
And men caught out in what the world
  Calls guilt, in first confusion

And almost every one when age,
  Disease, or sorrows strike him
Inclines to think that there is a God
  Or something very like him.

9

John Henry Newman on the Justification of Faith

John Henry Newman's major contribution to philosophy was his *Essay in Aid of a Grammar of Assent,*[1] published in 1870. This book centres upon a question of primary importance in the philosophy of religion: how can religious belief be justified, given that the evidence for its conclusions seems so inadequate to the degree of its commitment? The book contains much original material of interest on many philosophical topics. But on the precise question of the nature and justification of faith some of Newman's very best work occurs not here but in his earlier University

---

[1] John Henry Newman, *Essay in Aid of a Grammar of Assent,* ed. I.T. Ker (Oxford: Clarendon Press, 1985). (References hereafter to G.)

Sermons.[2] These sermons were preached between 1826 and 1843, between Newman's appointment as a college tutor in Oxford and his resignation of the living of the University Chuch of St Mary's, all of them while he was a Fellow of Oriel. There is no great difference in actual doctrine between Newman's Anglican and Catholic writings on this topic, and where there are differences they seem not to depend on religious or doctrinal grounds. There are at least as great differences between his earlier and later Oriel sermons as between the later Oriel sermons and the *Grammar*.

In the theological tradition in which Newman wrote, faith was contrasted on the one hand with reason and knowledge and on the other with hope and charity. 'Faith' was used in a narrower sense than 'belief'. Aristotle believed that there was a divine prime mover unmoved; but his belief was not faith in God. On the other hand, Marlowe's Faustus, on the verge of damnation, speaks of Christ's blood streaming in the firmament; he has lost hope and charity yet retains faith. So faith contrasts both with reason and with love. The special nature of the belief that is faith is that it is a belief in something as revealed by God; belief in a proposition on the word of God.

This is a Catholic not a Protestant view of the nature of faith. Newman held it already in his University Sermons.

---

[2] John Henry Newman, *Sermons, Chiefly on the Theory of Religious Belief, Preached before the University of Oxford*, 2nd edn (London: Rivington, 1844). (Hereafter *U*.)

The Word of Life is offered to a man; and on its being offered, he has Faith in it. Why? On these two grounds – the word of its human messenger, and the likelihood of the message. And why does he feel the message to be probable? Because he has a love for it, his love being strong, though the testimony is weak. He has a keen sense of the intrinsic excellence of the message, of its desirableness, of its likeness to what it seems to him divine goodness would vouchsafe did He vouchsafe any.[3]

Newman attacks the idea that reason judges both the evidence for and the content of revelation, and opposes the view that faith is just state of heart, a moral quality, of adoration and obedience. Faith is itself an intellectual quality, even though reason is not an indispensable preliminary to faith.[4]

What is the role of reason? We have direct knowledge of material things through the senses: we are sensible of the existence of persons and things, we are directly cognizant of them through the senses. (To think that we have faculties for direct knowledge of immaterial things is a form of enthusiasm; certainly we are not conscious of any such faculties.) The senses are the only instruments which we know to be granted to us for direct and immediate acquaintance with things external to us. Even our senses convey us but a little way out of ourselves: we have to be near things to touch them; we can neither see hear nor touch things past or future.[5]

[3] Ibid., p. 195.
[4] Ibid., p. 173.
[5] Ibid., pp. 197–8.

Now reason is that faculty of the mind by which this deficiency is supplied; by which knowledge of things external to us, of beings, facts, and events, is attained beyond the range of sense. It ascertains for us not natural things only, or immaterial only, or present only, or past or future; but, even if limited in its power, it is unlimited in its range . . . It reaches to the ends of the universe, and to the throne of God beyond them; it brings us knowledge, whether clear or uncertain, still knowledge, in whatever degree of perfection, from every side; but, at the same time, with this characteristic that it obtains it indirectly, not directly.[6]

Reason does not really perceive any thing; but is a faculty of proceeding from things that are perceived to things which are not. It is the faculty of gaining knowledge upon grounds given; and its exercise lies in asserting one thing because of some other thing. When its exercise is conducted rightly, it leads to knowledge; when wrongly, to apparent knowledge, to opinion and error.[7]

If this be reason, then faith, simply considered, is itself an exercise of reason, whether right or wrong. For example: 'I assent to this doctrine as true, because I have been taught it'; or 'because persons whom I trust say it was once guaranteed by miracles.' It 'must be allowed on all hands', says Newman, 'either that [faith] is illogical, or that the mind has some grounds which are not fully brought out when the process is thus

[6] Ibid., p. 199.
[7] Ibid.

exhibited'. The world says faith is weak; scripture says it is unearthly.[8] Faith is an act of reason, but of what the world would call weak, bad or insufficient reason, and that because it rests on presumption more and on evidence less.

Newman says it is true that nothing is true or right but what may be justified and in a certain sense proved by reason. But that does not mean that faith is grounded on reason; unless a judge can be called the origin as well as the justifier of the innocence of those who are brought before him.[9] On a popular view, reason requires strong evidence before assent, faith is content with weaker evidence. So Hume, Bentham and all those who like them think that faith is credulity. But in fact credulity is the counterfeit of faith, as scepticism is of reason.[10]

> Faith . . . does not demand evidence so strong as is necessary for . . . belief on the ground of Reason; and why? For this reason, because it is mainly swayed by antecedent considerations . . . previous notices, prepossessions, and (in a good sense of the word) prejudices. The mind that believes is acted upon by its own hopes, fears, and existing opinions . . . previously entertained principles, views, and wishes.[11]

Unbelievers say that a man is as little responsible for his faith as for his bodily functions; both are from

[8] Ibid., pp. 200–1.
[9] Ibid., p. 174.
[10] Ibid., p. 177.
[11] Ibid., pp. 179–80.

nature, and the will cannot make a weak proof a strong one.

> But love of the great Object of Faith, watchful attention to Him, readiness to believe Him near, easiness to believe Him interposing in human affairs, fear of the risk of slighting or missing what may really have come from Him; these are feelings not natural to fallen man, and they come only of supernatural grace; and these are the feelings which make us think evidence sufficient, which falls short of a proof in itself.[12]

Thus we can see how faith is and is not according to reason: taken together with the antecedent probability that providence will reveal himself, otherwise deficient evidence may be enough for conviction, even in the judgement of reason. 'That is, Reason, weighing evidence only, or arguing from external experience, is counter to Faith; but, admitting the full influence of the moral feelings, it concurs with it.'[13]

De facto this was how it all happened in the preaching of Christ and the apostles. It is wrong to think oneself a judge of religious truth without preparation of heart:

> Gross eyes see not; heavy ears hear not. But in the schools of the world the ways towards Truth are considered high roads open to all men, however disposed, at all times. Truth is to be approached without homage. Every one is considered on a level with his neighbour; or rather, the powers of the intellect, acuteness, sagacity, subtlety and depth, are

[12] Ibid., p. 185.
[13] Ibid., p. 187.

thought the guides into Truth. Men consider that they have as full a right to discuss religious subjects as if they were themselves religious. They will enter upon the most sacred points of Faith at the moment, at their pleasure – if it so happen, in a careless frame of mind, in their hours of recreation, over the wine cup. Is it wonderful that they so frequently end in becoming indifferentists?[14]

The mismatch between evidence and commitment, and the importance of previous attitudes, is to be observed not only in religious faith but in other cases of belief. We read reports in the newspapers; we know nothing of the evidence and we are unacquainted with the witnesses; yet we believe without asking for evidence:

> Did a rumour circulate of a destructive earthquake in Syria or the South of Europe, we should readily credit it; both because it might easily be true, and because it was nothing to us though it were. Did the report relate to countries nearer home, we should try to trace and authenticate it. We do not call for evidence till antecedent probabilities fail.[15]

Newman goes on to develop the theme that faith is not the only exercise of reason which, when critically examined, would be called unreasonable and yet is not so. Choice of sides in political questions, decisions for or against economic policies, tastes in literature: in all such cases if we measure people's grounds merely by the reasons they produce we have no difficulty in holding them up to ridicule, or even censure. So too

[14] Ibid., p. 190–91.
[15] Ibid., p. 180.

with prophecies of weather, judgements of character, and even theories of the physical world.[16]

However systematically we argue on any topic, there must ever be something assumed ultimately which is incapable of proof, and without which our conclusion will be as illogical as faith is apt to seem to men of the world. We trust our senses without proof; we rely implicitly on our memory, and that too in spite of its being obviously unstable and treacherous. We trust to memory for the truth of most of our opinions; the grounds on which we hold them not being at a given moment all present to our minds:

> It may be said that without such assumption the world could not go on: true, and in the same way the Church could not go on without Faith. Acquiescence in testimony, or in evidence not stronger than testimony, is the only method, so far as we see, by which the next world can be revealed to us.[17]

Moreover, the more precious a piece of knowledge is, the more subtle the evidence on which it is received:

> We are so constituted that if we insist upon being as sure as is conceivable, in every step of our course, we must be content to creep along the ground, and can never soar. If we are intended for great ends, we are called to great hazards; and whereas we are given absolute certainty in nothing, we must in all things choose between doubt and inactivity.[18]

[16] Ibid., p. 202.
[17] Ibid., pp. 206–7.
[18] Ibid., p. 208.

In the pursuit of power, of distinction in experimental science, or of character for greatness, we cannot avoid risk. Great objects exact a venture and sacrifice is the condition of honour; so

> even though the feelings which prompt us to see God in all things, and to recognize supernatural works in matters of the world, mislead us at times, though they make us trust in evidence which we ought not to admit, and partially incur with justice the imputation of credulity, yet a Faith which generously apprehends Eternal truth, though at times it degenerates into superstition, is far better than that cold, sceptical, critical tone of mind, which has no inward sense of an overruling, everpresent Providence, no desire to approach its God, but sits at home waiting for the fearful clearness of his visible coming, whom it might seek and find in due measure amid the twilight of the present world.[19]

> The mind ranges to and fro, and spreads out, and advances forward with a quickness which has become a proverb and a subtlety and versatility which baffle investigation. It passes on from point to point, gaining one by some indication, another on a probability; then availing itself of an association; then falling back on some received law; next seizing on testimony; then committing itself to some popular impression, or some inward instinct, or some obscure memory; and thus it makes progress not unlike a clamberer on a steep cliff, who, by quick eye, prompt hand, and firm foot, ascends how he knows not himself, by personal endowments and by practice, rather than by rule, leaving no

[19] Ibid., p. 213.

track behind him, and unable to teach another. It is not too much to say that the stepping by which great geniuses scale the mountains for truth is as unsafe and precarious to men in general as the ascent of a skilful mountaineer up a literal crag. It is a way which they alone can take; and its justification lies in its success.[20]

But how can one tell what is success in religious matters? On Newman's own account, there is a close similarity between faith and bigotry. In each case the grounds are conjectural, the issue is absolute acceptance of a certain message or doctrine as divine. Faith 'starts from probability, yet it ends in peremptory statements, if so be, mysterious, or at least beyond experience. It believes an informant amid doubt, yet accepts his information without doubt.'

The University Sermons do not really succeed in solving the problem, to which Newman returns in the *Grammar*: how is it that a proposition which is not, and cannot be, demonstrated, which at the highest can only be proved to be truth-like, not true, nevertheless claims and receives our unqualified adhesion?

Some philosophers, for example Locke, say that there can be no demonstrable truth in concrete matter, and therefore assent to a concrete proposition must be conditional. Probable reasoning can never lead to certitude. According to Locke, there are degrees of assent, and absolute assent has no legitimate exercise except as ratifying acts of intuition or demonstration.

[20] Ibid., pp. 252–3.

Locke gives, as the unerring mark of the love of truth, the not entertaining any proposition with greater assurance than the proofs it is built on will warrant. 'Whoever goes beyond this measure of assent, it is plain, receives not truth in the love of it, loves not truth for truth-sake, but for some other by-end.'[21]

This doctrine of Locke's is one of Newman's main targets of attack. In *The Development of Doctrine*[22] he says that the by-end may be the love of God. In the *Grammar* he claims that Locke's thesis is insufficiently empirical, too idealistic. Locke calls men 'irrational and indefensible if (so to speak) they take to the water, instead of remaining under the narrow wings of his own arbitrary theory.'

On Locke's view, says Newman, assent would simply be a mere reduplication or echo of inference, assent just another name for inference. But in fact the two do not always go together: one may be strong and the other weak. We often assent when we have forgotten the reasons for our assent. Reasons may still seem strong, and yet we do not any longer assent. Sometimes assent is never given in spite of strong and convincing arguments, perhaps through prejudice, perhaps through tardiness. Arguments may be better or worse, but assent either exists or not.[23]

Even in mathematics there is a difference between

---

[21] John Locke, *Essay on Human Understanding*, IV, xvi, p. 6.

[22] John Henry Newman, *The Development of Doctrine* (London: Sheed & Ward, 1960), Chapter 7, p. 2.

[23] Newman, G, pp. 110–12.

inference and assent. A mathematician would not assent to his own conclusions, on new and difficult ground, and in the case of abstruse calculations, however often he went over his work, till he had the corroboration of other judgements besides his own.[24]

In demonstrative matters assent excludes doubt. In concrete cases, we do not give doubtful assent, for there are instances where we assent a little and not much.

> Usually we do not assent at all. Every day, as it comes, brings with it opportunities for us to enlarge our circle of assents. We read the newspapers; we look through debates in Parliament, pleadings in the law courts, leading articles, letters of correspondents, reviews of books, criticism in the fine arts, and we either form no opinion at all upon the subjects discussed, as lying out of our line, or at most we have only an opinion about them . . . we never say that we give [a proposition] a degree of assent. We might as well talk of degrees of truth as degrees of assent.[25]

But there are unconditional assents on evidence short of intuition and demonstration. We all believe without any doubt that we exist; that we have an individuality and identity all our own; that we think, feel and act, in the home of our own minds.

> Nor is the assent which we give to facts limited to the range of self-consciousness. We are sure beyond all hazard of a mistake, that our own self is not the only being existing;

[24] Ibid., p. 127.
[25] Ibid., p. 115.

that there is an external world; that it is a system with parts and a whole, a universe carried on by laws; and that the future is affected by the past. We accept and hold with an unqualified assent, that the earth, considered as a phenomenon, is a globe; that all its regions see the sun by turns; that there are vast tracts on it of land and water; that there are really existing cities on definite sites, which go by the names of London, Paris, Florence and Madrid. We are sure that Paris or London, unless suddenly swallowed up by an earthquake or burned to the ground, is today just what it was yesterday, when we left it.[26]

Newman's favourite example of a firm belief on flimsy evidence is our conviction that Great Britain is an island. We believe this because we have been so taught in our childhood, and it is so in all the maps. We have never heard it contradicted or questioned; on the contrary, every person and every book we have come across took it for granted.

> Our whole national history, the routine transactions and current events of the country, our social and commercial system, our political relations with foreigners, imply it in one way or another. Numberless facts, or what we consider facts, rest on the truth of it; no received fact rests on its being otherwise . . .[27]

However, negative arguments and circumstantial evidence are not all, in such a matter, which we have a right to require. A higher kind of proof is possible:

[26] Ibid., p. 117.
[27] Ibid.

those who have circumnavigated the island have a right to be certain. But have we ever ourselves fallen in with anyone who has? Our conviction, considered from a logical point of view, is similar to the belief, so long and so widely entertained, that the earth was immovable, and the sun careered round it. Newman is not suggesting that our certitude about Great Britain's insularity is less than rational; he is only pointing out that no satisfactory proof of it could be analysed.[28]

Take another example. What are my grounds for thinking that I shall die? I am as certain of it as that I now live; but on what evidence? People say there is a law of death; but how many witnesses have told me their own experience of deaths, sufficient to establish a law? The most I can offer is a *reductio ad absurdum*. Can I point to anyone who has lived 200 years? What has become of past generations if they did not die? But this is a roundabout argument to a conclusion I already believe relentlessly.

> We laugh to scorn the idea that we had no parents though we have no memory of our birth; that we shall never depart this life, though we can have no experience of the future; that we are able to live without food, though we have never tried; that a world of men did not live before our time, or that that world has no history; that there has been no rise and fall of states, no great men, no wars, no revolutions, no art, no science, no literature, no religion.[29]

[28] Ibid., pp. 191–2.
[29] Ibid., p. 117.

On all these truths, Newman sums up, we have an immediate and unhesitating hold, 'nor do we think ourselves guilty of not loving truth for truth's sake, because we cannot reach them through a series of intuitive proposition . . . None of us can think or act without the acceptance of truths, not intuitive, not demonstrated, yet sovereign.'[30]

Philosophers like Locke do not really have misgivings about the truths they call in question. They do not mean to imply that there is even the shadow of a doubt that Great Britain is an island, but they remind us that there is no proof of the fact equal in form to the proof of a proposition of Euclid:

> in consequence they and we are all bound to suspend our judgement about such a fact, though it be in an infinitesimal degree, lest we should seem not to love truth for truth's sake. Having made their protest, they subside without scruple into that same absolute assurance of only partially proved truths, which is natural to the illogical imagination of the multitude.[31]

Newman makes a distinction between simple assent and complex assent. Simple assent is often unconscious. There are innumerable acts of assent which we make without reflection. But complex or reflex assent is what is meant by certitude: and it is certitude that is the characteristic manifestation of religious faith. Newman describes certitude in the following way:

[30] Ibid., p. 118.
[31] Ibid., p. 119.

It seems then that on the whole there are three conditions of certitude: that it follows on investigation and proof, that it is accompanied by a specific sense of intellectual satisfaction and repose, and that it is irreversible. If the assent is made without rational grounds, it is a rash judgement, a fancy, or a prejudice; if without the sense of finality, it is scarcely more than an inference; if without permanence, it is a mere conviction.[32]

But how can faith be certitude, if certitude follows on investigation? Does not investigation imply doubt, which conflicts with faith? To set about concluding a proposition is not *ipso facto* to doubt its truth: we may aim at inferring a proposition, while all the time we assent to it; we do not deny our faith because we become controversialists. Investigation is not enquiry; enquiry is indeed inconsistent with assent. It is sometimes complained of that a Catholic cannot enquire into the truth of his creed: of course he cannot if he would retain the name of believer.[33]

But may not investigation lead to giving up assent? Yes, it may; but 'my vague consciousness of the possibility of a reversal of my belief in the course of my researches, as little interferes with the honesty and firmness of that belief while those researches proceed, as the recognition of the possibility of my train's oversetting is an evidence of an intention on my part of undergoing so great a calamity'.[34]

[32] Ibid., p. 168.
[33] Ibid., p. 125.
[24] Ibid., p. 127.

Newman describes the specific feeling of certainty: a feeling of satisfaction and self-gratulation: 'The repose in self and in its object, as connected with self, which is characteristic of Certitude, does not attach to mere knowing, that is to the perception of things, but to the consciousness of having that knowledge'.[35]

Assents may and do change; certitudes endure. This is why religion demands more than an assent to its truth; it requires a certitude, or at least an assent which is convertible into certitude on demand. Belief does not necessarily imply a positive resolution in the party believing never to abandon the belief. It implies not an intention never to change but the utter absence of all thought, or expectation or fear of change.

Newman from time to time talks as if there is such a thing as false certitude: a state which differs from knowledge only in its truth value. But, he says, not altogether consistently, if the proposition is objectively true, 'then the assent may be called a perception, the conviction a certitude, the proposition or truth a certainty, or thing known, or a matter of knowledge, and to assent to it is to know'.[36]

Whether or not certitude entails truth, it is undeniable that to be certain of something involves believing in its truth. It follows that if I am certain of a thing, I believe it will remain what I now hold it to be, even though my mind should have the bad fortune to let it drop. If we are certain, we spontaneously reject

[35] Ibid., p. 134.
[36] Ibid., p. 128.

objections to our belief as idle; though the contra-dictory of a truth be brought back to mind by the pertinacity of an opponent, or a voluntary or involun-tary act of imagination, still that contradictory proposition and its arguments are mere phantoms and dreams. This is like the way the mind revolts from the supposition that a straight line is the longest distance between two points, or that Great Britain is in shape an exact square, or that I shall escape dying.[37]

Some may say we should never have this contempt-bringing conviction of anything; but if in fact 'a man has such a conviction, if he is sure that Ireland is to the West of England, or that the Pope is the Vicar of Christ, nothing is left to him, if he would be consistent, but to carry his conviction out into this magisterial intolerance of any contrary assertion'. Newman goes on to say: 'Whoever loses his conviction on a given point is thereby proved not to have been certain of it.'[38]

But is there any specific state or habit of thought, of which the distinguishing mark is immutability? On the contrary, any conviction, false as well as true, may last; and any conviction, true as well as false, may be lost. No line can be drawn between such real certitudes as have truth for their object, and apparent certitudes. There is no test of genuine certitude of truth. What looks like certitude always is exposed to the chance of turning out to be a mistake. Certitude does not admit

[37] Ibid., p. 130.
[38] Ibid., pp. 130 ff.

of an interior, immediate test, sufficient to discriminate it from false certitude.[39]

Newman correctly distinguishes certainty from infallibility. My memory is not infallible; I remember for certain what I did yesterday, but that does not mean that my memory is infallible. I am quite clear that two and two make four, but I often make mistakes in long addition sums. Certitude concerns a particular proposition, infallibility is a faculty or gift. It is possible to be certain that Victoria is queen, without claiming infallibility, as it is possible to do a virtuous action without being impeccable.[40]

But how can the secure repose of certitude be mine if I know, as I know too well, that before now I have thought myself certain when I was certain after all of an untruth? What happened once may happen again. Newman's answer is this: mistakes should make us more cautious, but even so grounds for caution may be overcome.

> Suppose I am walking out in the moonlight, and see dimly the outlines of some figure among the trees; – it is a man. I draw nearer, it is still a man; nearer still, and all hesitation is at an end, – I am certain it is a man. But he neither moves nor speaks when I address him; and then I ask myself what can be his purpose in hiding among the trees at such an hour. I come quite close to him and put out my arm. Then I find for certain that what I took for a man is but a singular shadow, formed by the falling of the moonlight on the

[39] Ibid., p. 145.
[40] Ibid., p. 147.

interstices of some branches or their foliage. Am I not to indulge my second certitude, because I was wrong in my first? Does not any objection, which lies against my second from the failure of my first, fade away before the evidence on which my second is founded.[41]

We do not dispense with clocks because from time to time they go wrong and tell untruly.

The sense of certitude may be called the bell of the intellect; and that it strikes when it should not is a proof that the clock is out of order, no proof that the bell will be untrustworthy and useless when it comes to us adjusted and regulated from the hands of the clockmaker.[42]

Certitude, for Newman, is a mental state; while certainty is a quality of propositions. Certitude is the recognition of propositions as true; it is our duty to exercise it at the bidding of reason, and, when reason forbids, to withhold. We must give our assent on the basis of inference; and the accuracy of an inference is a matter of the judgement of the individual reasoning agent.

We have to accept being the kind of things we are: beings which have to progress by inference and assent. The course of inference is ever more or less obscure, while assent is ever distinct and definite, yet one follows on the other; we have to accept this. Aristotle says that no code of laws or moral treatise maps out the path of individual virtue. So too with the controlling principle

[41] Ibid., p. 151.
[42] Ibid., p. 152.

in inferences. There are as many forms of practical wisdom as there are virtues. There is no one formula which is a working rule for poetry, medicine, politics; so too with ratiocination. In reasoning on any subject whatever which is concrete we proceed, as far indeed as we can, by the logic of language; but we are obliged to supplement it by the more subtle and elastic logic of thought.

How does Newman apply this to the evidences for religion? Christianity is a revelation, a message from God to man distinctly conveyed by his chosen instruments, and to be received as such a message. It is to be embraced as true on the grounds of its being divine, not as true on intrinsic grounds; it is to be maintained, not as probably or partially true, but as absolutely certain knowledge, certain in a sense in which nothing else can be certain, because it comes from Him who neither can deceive nor be deceived.[43]

With regard to the justification of religious belief, Newman gives up the intention of demonstrating either natural religion or Christianity.

> Not that I deny that demonstration is possible. Truth, certainly, as such, rests upon grounds intrinsically and objectively and abstractedly demonstrative, but it does not follow from this that the arguments producible in its favour are unanswerable and irresistible . . . The fact of revelation is in itself demonstrably true, but it is not therefore true irresistibly; else how comes it to be resisted?[44]

[43] Ibid., p. 250.
[44] Ibid., p. 264.

'For me', says Newman, 'it is more congenial to my own judgement to attempt to prove Christianity in the same informal way in which I can prove for certain that I have been born into this world, and that I shall die out of it'.[45]

Newman's proof will only work for those who are prepared for it, imbued with religious opinions and sentiments identified with natural religion. He assumes the falsehood of the opinions which 'characterize a civilized age'. The evidences 'presuppose a belief and perception of the divine Presence'. Newman does not stress miracles, but rather 'those coincidences and their cumulations which, though not in themselves miraculous, do irresistibly force upon us, almost by the law of our nature, the presence of the extraordinary agency of Him whose being we already acknowledge'.

As example Newman quotes the sudden death of a market woman following the utterance of a curse, and the fact of Napoleon's being defeated in Russia within two years of his being excommunicated by the Pope. These coincidences are indications, he says, to those who believe in a Moral Governor, of his immediate presence. But the greatest of these impressive coincidences is the whole history of Judaism and Christianity.

> If the history of Judaism is so wonderful as to suggest the presence of some special divine agency in its appointments and fortunes, still more wonderful and divine is the history

[45] Ibid.

of Christianity; and again it is more wonderful still, that two such wonderful creations should span almost the whole course of ages, during which nations and states have been in existence, and should constitute a professed system of continued intercourse between earth and heaven from first to last amid all the vicissitudes of human affairs. This phenomenon again carries on its face, to those who believe in a God, the probability that it has that divine origin which it professes to have.[46]

Christianity, Newman maintains, is addressed to minds which already believe in God and in a future judgement (this, he says, is 'the normal condition of human nature'). It proceeds by 'arguments too various for direct enumeration, too personal and deep for words, too powerful and concurrent for refutation'. One and the same teaching is in different aspects both object and proof, and elicits one complex act both of inference and assent.[47]

Given Newman's own description of the scope of his argument, one may ask: why should one believe in God and in a future judgement at all? In response to this question Newman makes his celebrated appeal to the testimony of conscience. He is not confident in the probative force of the traditional arguments to the existence of God from the nature of the physical world.

It is indeed a great question whether Atheism is not as

---

[46] Ibid., p. 283.
[47] Ibid., p. 316.

philosophically consistent with the phenomena of the physical world, taken by themselves, as the doctrine of a creative and governing Power. But, however this be, the practical safeguard against Atheism in the case of scientific enquirers is the inward need and desire, the inward experience of that Power, existing in the mind before and independently of their examination of His material world.[48]

Just as from a multitude of perceptions we construct the notion of an external world, so from the intimations of conscience we proceed to the notion of an external monitor, a Supreme Ruler and Judge.[49]

Conscience is a mental phenomenon as much as memory, reason, or the sense of the beautiful. It is a moral sense and a sense of duty; a judgement of the reason and a magisterial dictate, it has both a critical and judicial office. Conscience, considered as a moral sense, is an intellectual sentiment, but it is always emotional; therefore it involves recognition of a living object. Inanimate things cannot stir our affections, these are correlative with persons.

If, on doing wrong, we feel the same tearful, broken-hearted sorrow which overwhelms us on hurting a mother; if on doing right, we enjoy the same sunny serenity of mind, the same soothing, satisfactory delight which follows on our receiving praise from a father, we certainly have within us the image of some person, to whom our love and veneration look, in whose smile we find our happiness, for

[48] Newman, U, p. 186.
[49] Newman, G, p. 72.

whom we yearn, towards whom we direct our pleadings, in whose anger we are troubled and waste away. These feelings in us are such as require for their exciting cause an intelligent being . . .[50]

So far I have expounded Newman without criticizing him. I wish to end by stating briefly my own position on the issues on which he wrote so eloquently.

Newman begins his own criticism of Locke with the following words: 'I have so high a respect both for the character and the ability of Locke . . . that I feel no pleasure in considering him in the light of an opponent'.[51] The Oxford philosopher H.H. Price, writing on the topic of belief, said 'Let us follow this excellent example; for no one, and certainly no Oxford man, should criticise Newman without praising him . . . Newman is one of the masters of English prose. The power, and the charm, of his style are so compelling that the reader soon becomes their willing captive, and it seems ungrateful, almost ungracious, to question what has been so felicitously said.'[52]

One's reluctance to take a stand against Newman is increased by the fact that Newman puts the objections to his own views so marvellously well: indeed, he is often at this best when stating a position against which he intends to argue. Let us admire, for instance, the way in which he states the argument which is most likely to

[50] Ibid., p. 76.
[51] Ibid., p. 107.
[52] H. H. Price, *Belief* (London: Allen & Unwin, 1969), p. 133.

have occurred to those who have followed his defence of the justification of Christian belief.

> Antecedent probabilities may be equally available for what is true and what pretends to be true, for a revelation and its counterfeit, for Paganism, or Mahometanism, or Christianity. They seem to supply no intelligible rule for what is to be believed and what not; or how a man is to pass from a false belief to a true. If a claim of miracles is to be acknowledged because it happens to be advanced, why not for the miracles of India as well as for those of Palestine? If the abstract probability of a Revelation be the measure of genuineness in a given case, why not in the case of Mahomet as well as of the Apostles?[53]

The argument against Newman's position here could hardly be better put; and so it is in many other cases where Newman maintains implausible and contentious opinions. None the less, I cannot conclude without stating that Newman's account of the nature and justification of faith is wrong on a number of major points. I will list, without defending, five criticisms which can be made of his position.

1. First, despite what Newman says, assent does have degrees and this is true in religious matters as in others. This is something which Newman himself knows and admits when he is off his guard. There is a difference between an assent to a proposition without fear of its falsehood but with a readiness to examine contrary evidence and change one's mind, and an assent like Newman's certitude which condemns all objections

[53] Newman, U, p. 226.

which may be brought against it. Newman himself gives examples of adherence to propositions which do not fulfil the conditions of certitude. Some of these concern matters of religious belief.

> I may believe in the liquefaction of St Pantaleon's blood, and believe it to the best of my judgement to be a miracle, yet supposing a chemist offered to produce exactly the same phenomena under exactly similar circumstances by the materials put at his command by his science, so as to reduce what seemed beyond nature within natural laws, I should watch with some suspense of mind and misgiving the course of his experiment, as having no divine Word to fall back upon as a ground of certainty that the liquefaction was miraculous.[54]

This is a very important passage, which gives away Newman's official position. It shows that there is such a thing as belief, and indeed religious belief, which falls short of unconditional assent. The real question which Newman ought to be facing is this: why is not this kind of certitude the appropriate kind in religious matters, given the nature of the evidence for there being a divine revelation of Christianity?

2. Newman is right to emphasize, and it is one of his major contributions to philosophy, that a belief such as the belief that Great Britain is an island is not a belief based on sufficient evidence. But the reason for this is that it is not based on evidence at all. For evidence has to be better known than that for which it is evidence; and none of the scraps of reasons I could produce for

[54] Newman, G, p. 132.

the proposition that Great Britain is an island are better known than the proposition itself.

But this means that there is not the parallel which Newman drew between the belief that Great Britain is an island and the religious faith of a Christian believer. For faith to be faith and not mere belief it has to be belief on the word of God. If that is so, then the fact of revelation has to be better known than the content of revelation. But this Newman does not even attempt to prove.

3. Again, Newman is quite unconvincing in claiming that certitude is indefectible. It is true that knowledge is indefectible: if I claim to know that p, and then change my mind about p, I also withdraw the claim that I ever knew that p. But certainty is not like knowledge here: there is nothing odd in saying 'I was certain but I was wrong.' The difference between the two is connected with the fact that knowledge is only of what is true. But Newman agrees (though not with complete regularity) that there can be false certitude. Hence his position is internally inconsistent here.

However, the internal inconsistency in this case may not be very important given Newman's apologetic purpose. There is no sufficient reason for him to insist that certitude must be indefectible. Once Newman has shown, convincingly, that past mistakes do not make subsequent certainty impossible to justify, it is not of great moment whether certainties may be lost, and it becomes just a matter of the definition of certitude as contrasted with conviction. Newman, to his credit, does not ever argue 'I am certain, *ergo* this is true.'

4. Newman's argument from conscience is unconvincing. The parallel drawn in *Grammar* with our knowledge of the external world is based on a false phenomenalist view which most philosophers would now regard as indefensible. It is interesting that this view conflicts with that presented in the University Sermons. In his later, but not his earlier, writing Newman assumes that our knowledge of material objects is indirect, a hypothesis from phenomena.

5. Conscience itself may be seen as conditioned or absolute. If conditioned, it is the result of reasoning – as it is for the Utilitarian, operating his felicific calculus. Newman is aware of this, and denounces the idea. 'We reprobate under the name of Utilitarianism, the substitution of Reason for Conscience'.[55] But reasoning need not be Utilitarian, and Aristotle, whose practical wisdom Newman takes as the paradigm for the sense which leads us to assent to non-probative inferences, does present a theory of conscience which makes it the result of practical reasoning.

If, on the other hand, conscience is thought of not as a conclusion from reasoning but as an absolute dictate, then the objection of J.L. Mackie tells:

> If we take conscience at its face value and accept as really valid what it asserts, we must say that there is a rational prescriptivity about certain kinds of action for doing them or for refraining from them. There is a to-be-done-ness or a not-to-be-done-ness involved in that kind of action in itself. If so, there is no need to look beyond this to any

[55] Newman, *U*, p. 175.

supernatural person who commands or forbids such action . . .[56]

If the existence of God is looked on not as something perceived behind conscience but as something to explain the origin of conscience, then of course Newman's hypothesis needs to be considered in competition with other hypotheses. One such hypothesis is the theory of Freud, which to any modern reader is brought irresistibly to mind by the passage quoted above (p. 148) about the delight which results from the praise of a father.

One of the earliest readers of the *Grammar* was Gerard Manley Hopkins. He wrote to a friend: 'It is perhaps heavy reading. The justice and candour and gravity and rightness of mind is what is so beautiful in all he writes but what dissatisfies me is a narrow circle of instance and quotation . . . But he remains, nevertheless, our greatest living master of style.'[57]

Hopkins offered to write a commentary to remedy the deficiencies of the book. Given the smooth sunlit brilliance of most of Newman's writing, and the dense tangled opacity of which Hopkins was master, it is not surprising that Newman rejected the suggestion with a degree of asperity. But it would have been wonderful to have had a work which combined the gifts of the age's two greatest masters of English.

[56] J. L. Mackie, *The Miracle of Theism* (Oxford: Oxford University Press, 1982), p. 104.

[57] Gerard Manley Hopkins, *Further Letters*, ed. C.C. Abbot (London: Oxford University Press, 1956), p. 58.

10

Leslie Stephen and the Mountains of Truth

I first engaged with the thought of Stephen when, some years ago, I was compiling an anthology on the topic of mountains, and the human response to mountains, throughout the ages.[1] It was the theme of the anthology that the love of mountains was no new thing, no fad of an industrial era. Human beings, I claimed, have loved mountains since history began, but their love has taken different forms in different ages. In pursuing this theme I found myself constantly in collision with the interpretation placed on the history of mountains by Leslie Stephen

For it was Stephen who convinced the world that before the closing decades of the eighteenth century mankind in general hated mountains. The contrast which he drew between the old perception and the new was greatly overdrawn; both before and after the onset

[1] Anthony Kenny, *Mountains* (London: John Murray, 1991).

of the romantic era the relation of the human race to the mountains of its planet was a mixture of fear and love.

But while opposing Stephen's general view of the story I wanted my anthology to tell, I soon came to rank him among my favourite mountain writers. Several of the choicest specimens I selected for inclusion in the anthology were passages from his own works. For his book *The Playground of Europe*[2] occupies a significant position in the literature of the heyday of the Alps. The attitude expressed in the title and content of that book sets Stephen in opposition to the greatest of the Victorian mountain writers, John Ruskin.

Ruskin's love of mountains knew no bounds: for him, all natural beauty, all moral goodness, was to be judged by its proximity to or distance from the ideal serenity of the high peaks. For him the mountains were the great cathedrals of the earth. Ruskin's best descriptions of mountain scenery remain unsurpassed: but his passion for the mountains remained Platonic: he was a mountain-lover, but no mountaineer. Stephen, on the other hand, was a mountaineer before he was a writer. He was a better writer than most of the Victorian climbers, and a better climber than the best of the Victorian writers.

Ruskin believed that the spreading enthusiasm for Alpine climbing was leading to the ruin of Switzerland by people who regarded the country as half watering-

---

[2] Leslie Stephen, *The Playground of Europe* (London: Longmans, 1891).

place, half gymnasium. He denied that mountaineering enhanced one's appreciation of mountain beauty; instead, it deadened it.

> The real beauty of the Alps is to be seen, and seen only, where all may see it, the child, the cripple, and the man of grey hairs. There is more true loveliness in a single glade of pasture shadowed by pine, or gleam of rocky brook, or inlet of unsullied lake, among the lower Bernese and Savoyard hills, than in the entire field of jagged gneiss which crests the central ridge from the Schreckhorn to the Viso. The valley of Cluse, through which unhappy travellers consent now to be invoiced, packed in baskets like fish, so only that they may cheaply reach, in the feverous haste which has become the law of their being, the glen of Chamouni whose every lovely foreground rock has now been broken up to build hotels for them, contains more beauty in half a league of it, than the entire valley they have devastated, and turned into a casino, did in its uninjured pride; and that passage of the Jura by Olten (between Basle and Lucerne), which is by the modern tourist triumphantly effected through a tunnel in ten minutes, between two piggish trumpet grunts proclamatory of the ecstatic transit, used to show from every turn and sweep of its winding ascent, up which one sauntered, gathering wild-flowers for half a happy day, diviner aspects of the distant Alps than ever were achieved by toil of limb, or won by risk of life.[3]

So much for Stephen and his fellow members of the Alpine Club. But one thing was common to Ruskin and

---

[3] John Ruskin, *Sesame and Lilies* (London: George Allen, 1907), p. 166.

to the athletic climbers who aroused his disgust: they both valued the mountains as the antithesis of the city. The Victorian businessman, no less than the Desert Fathers, sought in the solitude of the mountains release and purification from the bustle of commercial and competitive life. Just as a third-century hermit might treasure the biblical texts which urged flight from the world, so too the nineteenth-century mountaineer would remind himself of Blake's dictum

> Great things are done when men and mountains meet
> That is not done by jostling in the street.

Or he would quote from Byron:

> I live not in myself, but I become
> Portion of that around me, and to me
> High mountains are a feeling, but the sum
> Of human cities torture.

The Christian hermit, however, went to the mountains for life, the Victorian man of letters went for a holiday. The novelty of the mid-nineteenth century, which Ruskin hated and blamed on men such as Stephen, was the emergence of mountaineering as a sport. Early mountaineers, if they were not to be thought frivolous or reckless, felt obliged to emphasize that their climbing was – like Petrarch's – an act of piety, or – like Saussure's – a pursuit of science. With the foundation of the Alpine Club in 1857 there were more and more Alpinists who were willing to admit frankly that they ascended the mountains for pleasure, in the pursuit of challenging, invigorating and increasingly competitive physical exercise. The Alps, once inaccessible, once forbidding, once sublime, turned by degrees into the playground of Europe. It was this that Ruskin hated, and this that Stephen defended.

Stephen was willing to join Ruskin in condemning the vulgarity which the popularity of the Alps brought. But he was prepared to claim that even from a strictly aesthetic point of view, the mountaineer has a greater appreciation of mountain scenery than the non-mountaineer.

> The qualities which strike every sensitive observer are impressed upon the mountaineer with tenfold force and intensity. If he is as accessible to poetical influences as his neighbours – and I don't know why he should be less so – he has opened new avenues of access between the scenery and his mind. He has learnt a language which is but partially revealed to ordinary men. But I know some sceptical critics will ask, does not the way in which he is accustomed to regard mountains rather deaden their poetical influence? Doesn't he come to look at them as mere instruments of sport, and overlook their more spiritual teaching? Does not all the excitement of personal adventure and the noisy apparatus of guides, and ropes, and axes, and tobacco, and the fun of climbing, rather dull his perceptions and incapacitate him from perceiving
>
> > The silence that is in the starry sky.
> > The sleep that is among the lonely hills?[4]

[4] Stephen, *The Playground of Europe*, p. 238.

In fact, Stephen maintained, what gives its inexpressible charm to mountaineering is the incessant series of exquisite natural scenes which are for the most part enjoyed by the mountaineer alone. He describes in vivid detail the glory of the sunrise on the Alpine summits as it gradually presents itself to the early morning climber ascending in the thin upper air.

> I might go on indefinitely recalling the strangely impressive scenes that frequently startle the traveller in the waste upper world; but language is feeble indeed to convey even a glimmering of what is to be seen to those who have not seen it for themselves, whilst to them it can be little more than a peg upon which to hang their own recollections. These glories, in which the mountain Spirit reveals himself to his true worshippers, are only to be gained by the appropriate service of climbing – at some risk, though a very trifling risk, if he is approached with due form and ceremony – into the furthest recesses of his shrines. And without seeing them, I maintain that no man has really seen the Alps.[5]

My topic in this essay is agnosticism, not mountaineering, and the reader may be wondering when I am going to get around to it. The two topics are not unconnected, for there were links between the Victorian passion for mountains and the Victorian ambivalence about religion. Matthew Arnold used the mountain scenery of the Grande Chartreuse as the setting for the most famous poetical expression of the Victorian crisis of faith. The geologist's hammer which was no less

[5] Ibid., p. 240.

essential than an ice-axe as a tool for the early nineteenth-century mountaineer was also the instrument which undermined the cosmic chronology of biblical fundamentalism. Those who abandoned Christian belief were anxious to exhibit, in the stoic traits of character essential for success above the snowline, that loss of faith need involve no diminution of moral fibre. Those who gave up belief in the eternal God of Abraham, Isaac and Jacob were glad to retain a sublime object of awe in the everlasting snows of Mont Blanc, Monte Rosa and the Matterhorn. John Tyndall, the agnostic President of the Royal Society, thus describes the view from the summit of the Weisshorn: 'An influence seemed to proceed from it direct to the soul; the delight and exultation experienced were not those of Reason or Knowledge, but of BEING: I was part of it and it of me, and in the transcendent glory of Nature I entirely forgot myself as man.' There was something incongruous, if not profane, he felt, 'in allowing the scientific faculty to interfere where silent worship was the "reasonable service" '.

Stephen had taken orders in the Church of England, rather lightheartedly it seems, and with a view to obtaining a fellowship, in 1855. By 1862 he had rejected Christianity, and ceased to attend chapel; in consequence he resigned his tutorship, though he was allowed to retain his fellowship until his marriage in 1867. He described his own position henceforth as agnostic, making popular the word which had been coined, rather obscurely, by Huxley in 1869. For the rest of this paper I want to discuss in some detail the position most succinctly expressed in his essay, 'An Agnostic's Apology', published in the *Fortnightly* and reprinted as the title essay of his collected essays on faith and scepticism in 1893.[6]

In an earlier essay (p. 8), I drew a distinction between positive and negative atheism. A negative atheist is an a-theist or non-theist in the sense of not being a theist or believer in the existence of God. But the negative atheist is not necessarily a positive atheist: she may lack not only a belief in the existence of God but also a belief in the non-existence of God.

The distinction between positive and negative atheism is not one which is used by Stephen, though I think it is useful in characterizing his own position. He avoids the word 'atheist' as having 'a certain flavour as of the stake in this world and hell-fire in the next'. He regards the word 'agnostic' as representing an advance in the courtesies of controversy. In the terms we have just set out, Stephen was a negative atheist; but in order to characterize accurately his position we need to make a further distinction within negative atheism. Those who lack the belief in God may do so either because they think that the statement 'God exists' is meaningful but uncertain, or because they think that the sentence is not really meaningful at all. Thus, one of the most celebrated nineteenth-century atheists, Charles Bradlaugh, expressed his own atheism thus: 'The Atheist does not

---

[6] Leslie Stephen, *An Agnostic's Apology and Other Essays* (London: Smith & Elder, 1893).

say "There is no God", but he says "I know not what you mean by God; I am without the idea of God; the word 'God' is to me a sound conveying no clear or distinct affirmation." ' The belief that religious language is meaningless has had considerable popularity among philosophers in the twentieth century; Stephen to some extent anticipated this position in his attack on religious dogma as being both unverifiable and empty in its claims. However, his main position is not that 'God exists' has no truth-value, but that its truth-value is unascertainable by human beings. To a contemporary reader of Stephen it is interesting to see how little the essentials of the debate about theism have changed, in spite of the many developments in logic and philosophy in the intervening hundred years.

Stephen defines the central position of agnosticism as being that there are limits to the sphere of human intelligence, and theology is within the forbidden sphere. The divines whom Stephen is attacking he nicknames 'Gnostics'. The gnostic holds that reason can transcend experience, and we can attain truths not capable of verification, and not needing verification, by actual experiment or observation. He holds that a knowledge of those truths is essential to the highest interests of mankind, and enables us in some sort to solve the dark riddle of the universe. But the gnostic's so-called knowledge is illusory, and the consolations offered by gnostics are mockeries. 'Pain is not an evil; death is not a separation; sickness is but a blessing in disguise. Have the gloomiest speculations of avowed pessimists ever tortured sufferers like those kindly platitudes? Is there a more cutting piece of satire in the language than the reference in our funeral service to the "sure and certain hope of a blessed resurrection"?[7]

Just as in his mountain writing Stephen came into conflict with the most gifted mountain writer of the age, so in his religious writing he came into conflict with the most gifted religious writer of the age: John Henry Newman. For among the gnostics whom he attacks there is none whom he cites more often, or treats with more respect, than Newman. The very title of his essay, 'An Agnostic's Apology' no doubt contains an allusion to Newman's *Apologia pro vita sua*, and from time to time he takes explicit issue with Newman's most important work of philosophy of religion, *Essays in Aid of a Grammar of Assent*.[8] In the rest of this essay I want to act as umpire in the argument between Stephen and Newman, using Stephen as spokesman for agnosticism, and Newman as spokesman for apologetics, that is, for the systematic attempt to show that religious belief is reasonable.

Newman's account of reason does, indeed, accord with Stephen's description of the gnostic. Newman agrees with Stephen that it is through the senses that we have direct knowledge of material things: we are sensible of the existence of persons and things; we are directly cognizant of them through the senses. It is reason that

[7] Ibid., p. 66.

[8] John Henry Newman, *Essays in Aid of a Grammar of Assent*, ed. I.T. Ker (Oxford: Clarendon Press, 1985). (References hereafter to G.)

takes us beyond our immediate environment to reach out to the ends of the universe and beyond.

Newman's explanation of the relationship between faith and reason goes as follows. Faith is itself an exercise of reason, and in a sense it must be proved and justified by reason, but it is not grounded on reason. It does not demand evidence as strong as reason does, because it is swayed, and rightly swayed, by antecedent considerations. The great problem with faith is this: that it is an irrevocable assent given on grounds which are less than logically compelling. Newman's regular defence of the apparent irrationality of this is to insist that there are many other unconditional assents on evidence short of intuition and demonstration. We all believe without any doubt that we exist; that we have an individuality and identity all our own; that we think, feel and act in the home of our own minds. We all believe that Great Britain is an island, and that each and every one of us was born of human parents and will one day die. But the evidence we have in support of these beliefs is far from probative.

Newman develops with great art the theme that faith is not the only exercise of the mind which, when critically examined, appears unreasonable and yet is not so. The more precious a piece of knowledge is, the more subtle the evidence on which it is received. To illustrate this Newman uses a metaphor which would appeal to Stephen

> We are so constituted that if we insist upon being as sure as is conceivable, in every step of our course, we must be

content to creep along the ground, and can never soar . . .
The mind ranges to and fro, and spreads out, and advances
forward with a quickness which has become a proverb and a
subtlety and versatility which baffle investigation. It passes
on from point to point, gaining one by some indication,
another on a probability; then availing itself of an association; then falling back on some received law; next seizing
on testimony; then committing itself to some popular
impression, or some inward instinct, or some obscure
memory; and thus it makes progress not unlike a clamberer
on a steep cliff, who, by quick eye, prompt hand, and firm
foot, ascends how he knows not himself, by personal
endowments and by practice, rather than by rule, leaving
no track behind him, and unable to teach another. It is not
too much to say that the stepping by which great geniuses
scale the mountains for truth is as unsafe and precarious to
men in general as the ascent of a skilful mountaineer up a
literal crag. It is a way which they alone can take; and its
justification lies in its success.[9]

But how can one tell what is success in religious
matters? On Newman's own account, there is a close
similarity between faith and bigotry. In each case the
grounds are conjectural, the issue is absolute acceptance of a certain message or doctrine as divine. Faith
'starts from probability, yet it ends in peremptory
statements, if so be, mysterious, or at least beyond
experience. It believes an informant amid doubt, yet
accepts his information without doubt.'

[9] J.H. Newman, *Sermons, Chiefly on the Theory of Religious
Belief, Preached before the University of Oxford*, 2nd edn (London:
Rivington, 1844) (hereafter *U*), pp. 252–3.

Newman is right to emphasize, in arguing in favour of belief in the absence of proof, that a belief such as the belief that Great Britain is an island is not a belief based on sufficient evidence. But the reason for this is that it is not based on evidence at all. For evidence has to be better known than that for which it is evidence; and none of the scraps of reasons I could produce for the proposition that Great Britain is an island are better known than the proposition itself. But this means that there is not the parallel which Newman drew between the belief that Great Britain is an island and the religious faith of a Christian believer. For faith to be faith and not mere belief it has to be belief on the word of God. If that is so, then the fact of revelation has to be better known than the content of revelation. But this Newman does not prove, nor even seriously attempt to do so.

For our purposes, we need not go into the details of how Newman seeks to present the apologetic argument for the truth of Christianity. For Newman agrees that to follow his argument there are two prerequisities; and Stephen, in disputing with Newman, attacks these prerequisites rather than the apologetic argument itself.

Newman's proof, he says will only work for those who are prepared for it, imbued with religious opinions and sentiments identified with natural religion. He assumes the falsehood of the opinions which 'characterize a civilized age'.[10] The evidences 'presuppose a

---

[10] Ibid., pp. 190–91.

belief and perception of the divine Presence'.[11] Above all, a particular frame of mind is required. It is wrong to think oneself a judge of religious truth without preparation of heart.

> Gross eyes see not; heavy ears hear not. But in the schools of the world the ways towards Truth are considered high roads open to all men, however disposed, at all times. Truth is to be approached without homage. Every one is considered on a level with his neighbour; or rather, the powers of the intellect, acuteness, sagacity, subtlety and depth are thought the guides into Truth. Men consider that they have as full a right to discuss religious subjects, as if they were themselves religious.[12]

Stephen regards the gnostic's appeal to preparation of heart as being a subtle form of pride. Can the gnostic prove his dogmas? Have they any meaning?

> The Gnostics rejoice in their knowledge. Have they anything to tell us? They rebuke what they call the 'pride of reason' in the name of a still more exalted pride. The scientific reasoner is arrogant because he sets limits to the faculty in which he trusts, and denies the existence of any other faculty. They are humble because they dare to tread in the regions which he declares to be inaccessible.[13]

Divines say they intuit God; Stephen avows that he does not.

---

[11] Ibid.
[12] Ibid.
[13] Stephen, *Agnostic's Apology*, p. 20.

Then says the divine, I can't prove my statements, but you would recognize their truth if your heart or your intellect were not corrupted: that is, you must be a knave or a fool. This is a kind of argument to which one is perfectly accustomed in theology. I am right, and you are wrong; and I am right because I am good and wise. By all means; and now let us see what your wisdom and goodness can tell us.[14]

Stephen mocks at the arrogance of the gnostics, and one might go further and argue that their arrogance is no accident. I have argued in an earlier essay (p. 102) that faith, credal faith, is incompatible with humility. The virtue of rationality marks the just mean between believing too much (credulity) and believing too little (scepticism). From the viewpoint of the agnostic both the theist and the atheist err by credulity; from the point of view of theism, the agnostic errs on the side of scepticism. On purely cognitive grounds there is no way of settling whether it is the agnostic who errs on the side of scepticism, or the theist who is erring on the side of credulity. But it is clear that the agnostic is humbler than the gnostic: the theist is claiming to be in possession of information, while the agnostic lays claim only to ignorance.

Stephen objects in particular to believers who simply presuppose the existence of God. Newman observes: 'Christianity is addressed, both as regards its evidences and its contents, to minds which are in the normal

[14] Ibid., p. 30.

169

condition of human nature, as believing in God and in a future judgement.'[15] Given Newman's own description of the scope of his argument, one may ask: Why should one believe in God and in a future judgement at all? In response to this question Newman makes his celebrated appeal to the testimony of conscience. He is not confident in the probative force of the traditional arguments to the existence of God from the nature of the physical world. 'It is indeed a great question whether Atheism is not as philosophically consistent with the phenomena of the physical world, taken by themselves, as the doctrine of a creative and governing Power.'[16]

Stephen seizes on this. Newman, he says,

holds that the unassisted reason cannot afford a sufficient support for a belief in God. He declares, as innumerable writers of less power have declared, that there is 'no medium, in true philosophy, between Atheism and Catholicity, and that a perfectly consistent mind, under those circumstances in which it finds itself here below, must embrace either the one or the other'.[17]

He continues:

The very basis of orthodox theology is the actual separation of the creation from the Creator. In the *Grammar of Assent* Newman tells us that we 'can only glean from the surface of the world some faint and fragmentary

[15] Newman, *G*, p. 316.
[16] Newman, *U*, p. 186.
[17] Stephen, *Agnostic's Apology*, p. 11.

views of God.' 'I see', he proceeds, 'only a choice of alternatives in view of so critical a fact, either there is no Creator, or he has disowned His creatures.' The absence of God from His own world is the one prominent fact which startles and appals him. Newman of course does not see or does not admit the obvious consequence. He asserts most emphatically that he believes in the existence of God as firmly as in his own existence; and he finds the ultimate proof of this doctrine – a proof not to be put into mood and figure – in the testimony of the conscience. But he apparently admits that Atheism is as logical, that is, as free from self-contradiction, as Catholicism.[18]

Newman's theism can only be supported by his Catholicity; so if, like three-quarters of mankind, he had never heard of Catholicism, he ought logically to be an atheist.

Stephen lays emphasis on the differences between competing religions. Whether we take natural or revealed religion, there is the difficulty of the contradictions between antagonistic beliefs. This difficulty was candidly stated by Newman himself when he admitted that antecedent probabilities might be equally available for what is true and what pretends to be true, for a revelation and its counterfeit, for Paganism, or Mahometanism, or Christianity. 'If a claim of miracles is to be acknowledged because it happens to be advanced, why not for the miracles of India as well as for those of Palestine? If the abstract probability of a

[18] Ibid.

Revelation be the measure of genuineness in a given case, why not in the case of Mahomet as well as of the Apostles?'[19]

The race collectively, Stephen argues, is agnostic, whatever may be the case with individuals. Newman may be as much convinced of the truth of his theology as Professor Huxley of its error.

> But speaking of the race, and not of the individual, there is no plainer fact in history than the fact that hitherto no knowledge has been attained. There is not a single proof of natural theology of which the negative has not been maintained as vigorously as the affirmative ... State any one proposition in which all philosophers agree, and I will admit it to be true; or any one which has a manifest balance of authority, and I will agree that it is probable. But so long as every philosopher flatly contradicts the first principles of his predecessors, why affect certainty? The only agreement I can discover is, that there is no philosopher of whom his opponents have not said that his opinions lead logically either to Pantheism or to Atheism.[20]

> The very hopelessness of the controversy shows that the reasoners have been transcending the limits of reason. They have reached a point where, as at the pole, the compass points indifferently to every quarter. Thus there is a chance that I may retain what is valuable in the chaos of specula-tion, and reject what is bewildering by confining the mind to its proper limits. But has any limit ever been suggested,

[19] Newman, *U*, p. 226.
[20] Stephen, *Agnostic's Apology*, p. 15. Subsequent quotations are from pp. 16–39, *passim*.

except a limit which comes in substance to an exclusion of all ontology? In short, if I would avoid utter scepticism, must I not be an Agnostic?

Now Stephen moves in for the kill: Gnosticism is either empty or self-contradictory. This remains true whether you explore the pantheistic or the libertarian solution to the problems we have been considering.

Let us allow for sake of argument that theologians can argue beyond experience. What then? 'Admit that the mind can reason about the Absolute and the Infinite, and you will get to Spinoza. Theology, if logical, leads straight to Pantheism. The Infinite God is everything. All things are bound together as cause and effect. God, the first cause, is the cause of all effects down to the most remote.' But if you accept Spinoza, you have to reject revelation; and pantheism gives no ground for morality, for nature causes evil and vice as much as it causes good and virtue.

> The attempt to transfer to pure being or to the abstraction Nature the feelings with which we are taught to regard a person of transcendent wisdom and benevolence is, as theologians assert, hopeless. To deny the existence of God is in this sense the same as to deny the existence of no-God. We keep the old word; we have altered the whole of its contents. A Pantheist is, as a rule, one who looks upon the universe through his feelings instead of his reason, and who regards it with love because his habitual frame of mind is amiable. But he has no logical argument as against the Pessimist, who regards it with dread unqualified by love, or the Agnostic, who finds it impossible to regard it with any but a colourless emotion.

Next, Stephen takes up the issue of freedom and determinism. The gnostic cannot be a consistent pantheist because he believes in free will. Pantheism involves universal causation; free will implies that the class of phenomena most important to us are not caused.

> An uncaused phenomenon is unthinkable; yet conscious-ness testifies that our actions, so far as they are voluntary, are uncaused. In face of such a contradiction, the only rational state of mind is scepticism. A mind balanced between two necessary and contradictory thoughts must be in a hopeless state of doubt. The Gnostic, therefore, starts by proclaiming that we must all be Agnostics in regard to a matter of primary philosophical importance. If by free-will he means anything else than a denial of causation, his statement is irrelevant.

The problem of free will is not a matter of refined speculation but affects practical knowledge.

> The determinist asserts, whilst the libertarian denies, that it would be possible for an adequate intelligence to foretell the actions of a man or a race. There is or is not an element of objective chance in the question; and whether there is or is not must be decided by reason and observation . . . The anti-determinist asserts the existence of chance so positively, that he doubts whether God himself can foretell the future of humanity; or, at least, he is unable to reconcile divine prescience with his favourite doctrine. In most practical questions, indeed, the difference is of little importance. The believer in free-will admits that we can make an approximate guess; the determinist admits that our faculty of calculation is limited.

174

But free will is made responsible, by the gnostic, for the moral evil in the world; hence all this evil is result of accident; no man could have foretold it. Here then is agnosticism in highest degree: it is impossible for us to say whether this world is ante-room to heaven or hell.

> The Gnostic invites us to rejoice because the existence of an infinitely good and wise Being has left it to chance whether His creatures shall all, or in any proportion, go straight to the devil. He reviles the Calvinist, who dares to think that God has settled the point by his arbitrary will. Is an arbitrary decision better or worse than a trusting to chance? We know that there is a great First Cause; but we add that there are at this moment in the world some twelve hundred million little first causes which may damn or save themselves as they please.

The free will hypothesis is necessary not only to relieve God from responsibility for suffering, but to enable him to be the judge of human doing and mis-doing. 'Man must be partly independent of God, or God would be at once pulling the wires and punishing the puppets.'

Stephen turns to the problem of Job: why do the good so often suffer, and the evil so often flourish? The difficulty, says the determinist, arises entirely from applying the conception of justice where it is mani-festly out of place. The advocate of free will refuses this escape, and is perplexed by a further difficulty. Why are virtue and vice arbitrarily distributed?

> Of all the puzzles of this dark world, or of all forms of the one great puzzle, the most appalling is that which meets us

at the corner of every street. Look at the children growing up amidst moral poison; see the brothel and the public-house turning out harlots and drunkards by the thousand; at the brutalised elders preaching cruelty and shamelessness by example; and deny, if you can, that lust and brutality are generated as certainly as scrofula and typhus ... Will God damn all these wretches for faults due to causes as much beyond their power as the shape of their limbs or as the orbits of the planets?

If God makes no allowances, he is unjust; but if he judges on effort not performance, then virtue is degraded. 'Virtue is a reality precisely in so far as it is a part of nature, not of accident; or our fate, not of our free-will'. If happiness is a natural consequence of virtue, then we may hope that the virtuous will be happy hereafter; but if heaven is an arbitrary bonus, analogies break down.

The new world is summoned into being to redress the balance of the old. The fate which here too often makes the good miserable and the bad happy, which still more strangely fetters our wills and forces the strong will into wickedness and strengthens the weak will to goodness, will then be suspended. The motive which persuades us to believe in the good arrangement hereafter is precisely the badness of this ... The world is so chaotic that according to theologians, infinite rewards and penalties are required to square the account and redress the injustice here accumu-lated. What is this, so far as the natural reason is concerned, but the very superlative of Agnosticism?

It is all a mystery; and what is mystery but the theological phrase for agnosticism?

176

The believers who desire to soften away the old dogmas – in other words, to take refuge from the unpleasant results of their doctrine with the Agnostics, and to retain the pleasant results with the Gnostics – have a different mode of escape. They know that God is good and just; that evil will some- how disappear and apparent injustice be somehow redressed. The practical objection to this amiable creed suggests a sad comment upon the whole controversy. We fly to religion to escape from our dark forebodings. But a religion which stifles these forebodings always fails to satisfy us. We long to hear that they are groundless. As soon as we are told that they are groundless we mistrust our authority . . . There is a deep sadness in the world. Turn and twist the thought as you may, there is no escape . . .

This view is based on feeling, not knowledge.

The awe with which they regard the universe, the tender glow of reverence and love with which the bare sight of nature affects them, is to them the ultimate guarantee of their beliefs. Happy those who feel such emotions! Only, when they try to extract definite statements of fact from these impalpable sentiments, they should beware how far such statements are apt to come into terrible collision with reality . . . Of all questions that can be asked, the most important is surely this: Is the tangled web of this world composed chiefly of happiness or of misery? And of all questions that can be asked, it is surely the most unanswerable.

It cannot be settled a priori that misery or happiness predominates; that is as hopeless a task as to deduce from the principle of the excluded middle the distance from St Paul's to Westminster Abbey. Questions of fact can only be solved by examining facts.

> Perhaps such evidence would show – and if a guess were worth anything, I should add that I guess that it would show – that happiness predominates over misery in the composition of the known world. I am, therefore, not prejudiced against the Gnostic's conclusion; but I add that the evidence is just as open to me as to him.

Stephen's argument from inconsistency and contradiction may seem to show the futility of philosophy no less than of divinity. I believe that his account of the nature of philosophical disagreement is misconceived, but it would take a different essay to establish that point. What is important in the present context is that there is a great difference between the kind of assent that is invited by a philosopher and the kind of assent that is demanded by an evangelist. Stephen's fundamental quarrel is not so much with the content of the creed as with the imperiousness of its demand for belief. His final question is this: 'Why, when no honest man will deny in private that every ultimate problem is wrapped in the profoundest mystery, do honest men proclaim in pulpits that unhesitating certainty is the duty of the most foolish and ignorant?'

11

Wittgenstein on Mind and Metaphysics

Wittgenstein is often regarded as being both positivist and behaviourist: positivist in rejecting all metaphysics, and behaviourist in denying inner human life. So far as concerns philosophy of mind, this view is based on a misunderstanding of Wittgenstein's work. He did indeed attack one particular metaphysical theory of mind: the Cartesian theory. Cartesianism is metaphysical in the sense of isolating statements about mental life from any possibility of verification or falsification in the public world. But much of Wittgenstein's work in philosophy of mind is devoted to showing the importance of distinctions between different kinds of potentiality and actuality. These distinctions were one of the major concerns of the work of Aristotle which was the first book to bear the name *Metaphysics* and were a main target of classical anti-metaphysicians. In this sense Wittgenstein himself had a metaphysics of mind; and the metaphysical sensitivity which he shared with Aristotle was what enabled him to reject Cartesianism without falling in to behaviourism. In this essay I will try to illustrate different forms of metaphysics, and sketch Wittgenstein's attitude to each.

In his mature writings, Wittgenstein does not often speak of metaphysics. The word 'metaphysical' occurs only twice in the *Philosophical Investigations*.[1] In each case it has a pejorative sense. And Wittgenstein can sum up his method as being a corrective to metaphysics:

> When philosophers use a word – 'knowledge', 'being', 'object', 'I', 'proposition', 'name' – and try to grasp the *essence* of the thing, one must always ask oneself: is the word ever actually used in this way in the language which is its original home?
>   What *we* do is to bring words back from their metaphysical to their everyday use.[2]

Metaphysics here seems to be identified with the search for essences. But there can be a legitimate attempt to understand essences, on which Wittgenstein himself is engaged: 'We too in these investigations are trying to understand the essence of language – its function, its structure.'[3]

What is wrong is to consider the essence not as something which lies open to view and must merely be

[1] Ludwig Wittgenstein, *Philosophical Investigations* (Oxford: Blackwell, 1953).
[2] Ibid., 1, 116.
[3] Ibid., 92.

given a perspicuous description but as something interior and hidden: a kind of metaphysical clockwork or hardware which explains the functioning of mind and language.

The kind of metaphysics that Wittgenstein systematically attacks is the metaphysics which consists of grammar masquerading as science. One source of metaphysics is the philosopher's temptation to mimic the claims and methods of science. Metaphysics, in this sense, is a quasi physics, an imaginary physics elevated into something sublime and mysterious. The tendency to create this kind of metaphysics is well described in *Philosophical Investigations*, where Wittgenstein is talking about ostensive definition:

> We do here what we do in a host of similar cases: because we cannot specify any *one* bodily action which we call pointing to the shape (as opposed, for example, to the colour) we say that a *spiritual* activity corresponds to these words.
>
> When our language suggests a body and there is none: there, we should like to say, is a *spirit*.[4]

In allusion to this passage, we might call this kind of metaphysics 'spiritualistic metaphysics'. The passage already cited in which Wittgenstein describes the task of the philosopher as being to bring back words from their metaphysical usage itself comes in a section where Wittgenstein has been talking about the tendency to think of the proposition as something sublime, to put

[4] Ibid., 36.

a halo around thought, to think of logic as a structure of crystalline purity.[5] We think of the mind as a mysterious medium different from a physical medium where the strict laws of logic operate.

Let us look at some examples of spiritualistic metaphysics of the kind which was Wittgenstein's target. The metaphysical impulse may lead us to postulate spiritual substances, or spiritual processes. In each case we are misled by grammar: where it makes us expect a physical substance but there is not one, we invent a metaphysical substance; where it makes us expect an empirical process but we cannot find one, we postulate a incorporeal process.[6]

First, metaphysical substances. One of the most bizarre, as well as the most ubiquitous, misunderstandings of the nature of the mind is the picture of mind's relation to body as that between a little man or homunculus on the one hand and a tool or instrument on the other. We smile when medieval painters represent the death of the Virgin Mary by showing a small scale-model virgin emerging from her mouth, but basically the same idea can be found in the most unlikely places.

Descartes, when first he reported the occurrence of retinal images, warned us not to be misled by the resemblance between images and their objects into thinking that when we saw the object we had another pair of eyes, inside the brain, to see the images. But

[5] Ibid., 74–108.
[6] Ibid., 339.

he himself believed that seeing was to be explained by saying that the soul encountered an image in the pineal gland. This was a particularly striking version of what has been nicknamed 'the homunculus fallacy': the attempt to explain human experience and behaviour by postulating a little man within an ordinary man.

We humans are always inclined to explain things we only imperfectly understand in terms of the most advanced technology of the age in which we live. As time passes and technology progresses, the tool or instrument which the manikin is fancied to control gets more and more sophisticated. Thus Plato thought that the soul in its relation to the body could be compared with a sailor in a boat or a charioteer holding the reins. Many centuries later, Coleridge said that what poets meant by the soul was 'a being inhabiting our body and playing upon it, like a musician enclosed in an organ whose keys were placed inwards'.[7] More recently, the mind has been compared to a signalman pulling the signals in his signal-box, or the telephone operator dealing with the incoming and outgoing calls in the brain. Most recently, the boat, the chariot, the railroad and the telephone exchange have given way to the computer, so that the relation of the soul to the body is envisaged as that of the programmer who writes the software to the hardware which executes the program.

What is wrong with the homunculus fallacy? In itself there is nothing misguided in speaking of images in the brain, if one means patterns in the brain which can

[7] Samuel Taylor Coleridge, *Letters*, Vol. 1 (ed. E.L. Griggs, OUP 1955), p. 278.

be mapped onto features of the sensory environment. There is nothing philosophically objectionable in the suggestion that these schematic images may be observable to the neurophysiologist investigating the brain. What is misleading is to say that these images are visible to the soul, and that seeing consists in the soul's perception of these images.

The misleading aspect is that such an account pretends to explain seeing, but the explanation reproduces exactly the puzzling features which it was supposed to explain. For it is only if we think of the relation between a soul and an image in the pineal gland as being just like the relation between a human being and pictures seen in the environment that we will think that talk of an encounter between the soul and the image has any illuminating power at all. As a metaphor, manikin talk may be no more than a harmless necessary fancy; but as an element in a theory a manikin bedevils understanding. For whatever needs explaining in the behaviour of the man turns up, grinning and unexplained, in the shape of the manikin.

From an example of a metaphysical substance, let us turn to considering metaphysical processes. Wittgenstein discusses the question: Is understanding a mental process?[8] Some philosophers have thought that understanding was a psychological process in the same sense as we might call 'a psychological process' the reciting of a poem in one's head. But reflection soon shows that this is not so.

[8] Wittgenstein, *Philosophical Investigations*, 1, 151ff.

If meaning was a mental process accompanying the utterance of a sentence, it should be possible for the process of meaning to take place without the sentence being uttered at all. Can one, in fact, perform the act of meaning without uttering the sentence? If you try to do so, you are likely to find yourself reciting the sentence itself under your breath. But of course it would be absurd to suggest that simultaneously with every public utterance of a sentence there is a private one too: it would surely take great skill to ensure that the two processes were exactly synchronized with each other! And how terrible if the two came slightly out of synchrony, so that the meaning of one word got mistakenly attached to the next one!

Moreover, the question whether somebody understands a sentence, and whether she really means it, can be raised about sentences uttered in the privacy of the imagination no less than about sentences uttered before a public audience. Infuriated by a curmudgeonly relation, I may mutter to myself 'I wish he would drop dead!' Luckily, I don't mean it. I hum in my mind a Russian folk-song, enchanted by the sound of the words. But I haven't the faintest idea what they mean. If understanding and meaning were processes, they would have to accompany private utterances as well as public utterances. So if the processes involved were some kind of inner utterance, we would be set off on an endless quest for the real understanding.

Some philosophers have thought that understanding was a mental process in rather a different sense. They have conceived the mind as a hypothetical mechanism postulated to explain the observable intelligent behaviour of human beings. If one conceives the mind in this way one thinks of a mental process not as something comparable to reciting the ABC in one's head but as a process occurring in the special mental machinery. The process on this view is a mental process because it takes place in a medium which is not physical; the machinery operates according to its own mysterious laws, within a structure which is not material but spiritual; it is not accessible to empirical investigation, and could not be discovered, say, by opening up the skull of a thinker.

Such processes need not, on this view, be accessible either to the inner eye of introspection: the mental mechanism may operate too swiftly for us to be able to follow all its movements, like the pistons of a railway engine or the blades of a lawn-mower. But we may feel that if only we could sharpen our faculty for introspection, or somehow get the mental machinery to run in slow motion, we might be able actually to observe the processes of meaning and understanding.

According to one version of the mental-mechanism doctrine, understanding the meaning of a word consists in calling up an appropriate image in connection with it. In general, of course, we have no such experience when we use a word, and in the case of many words (such as 'the', 'if' 'impossible', 'one million') it is difficult even to suggest what would count as an appropriate image. But let us waive these points, allow that perhaps we can have images in our mind without noticing that we do, and consider only the kind of word for which this account sounds most plausible, such as colour words. We may examine the suggestion that in order to understand the order 'Bring me a red flower' one must have a red image in mind, and that it is by comparison with this image that one ascertains which flower to bring. This cannot be right: otherwise how could one obey the order 'imagine a red patch'? Whatever problems there are about identifying the redness of the flower recur with identifying the redness of the patch.

It is of course true that when we talk mental images often do pass through our minds. But it is not they which confer meanings on the words we use. It is rather the other way round: the images are like the pictures illustrating a text in the book. In general it is the text which tells us what the pictures are of, not the pictures which tell us what the words of the text mean.

In fact, understanding cannot be thought of as a process at all. Understanding is kind of ability, and therefore is a state rather than a process.[9] In so far as the exercise of understanding is an exercise of intelligence, we may call understanding a mental state. But it is important to guard against misunderstanding here. Understanding may be a mental state, but it is not a psychological state like pain or depression or excitement. Such states last over periods, and can be continuous or interrupted; but one cannot know uninterruptedly what a word means.

[9] Ibid., 59.

Wittgenstein's treatment of the many-faceted illusion that understanding is a mental process is an example of his critique of spiritualistic metaphysics. He attacks metaphysics not by the blunt instrument of some positivistic verification principle but by the careful drawing of distinctions which enable him to disentangle the mixture of truism and nonsense in the metaphysician's concept of mind.

Besides spiritualistic metaphysics, there is another kind of metaphysics to which Wittgenstein was implacably opposed. This is the view that there is a fundamental branch of philosophy which underlies and underpins the rest of philosophy and the rest of the sciences. We might call this kind of metaphysics 'foundationalist metaphysics'. Descartes, who was the arch-exponent of spiritualistic metaphysics, can also be taken as a spokesman for foundationalist metaphysics. 'The whole of philosophy', he wrote, 'is like a tree, whose roots are metaphysics, whose trunk is physics, and whose branches are all the other sciences.'[10] Not only Descartes, but many other thinkers have seen philosophy as an ordered system; a system which could perhaps be most perspicuously displayed by being cast into axiomatic form, as Spinoza tried to do.

Wittgenstein's *Tractatus*[11] has reminded many people of Spinoza; but his later philosophy was the very

[10] AT, VIII, p. 3.

[11] Ludwig Wittgenstein, *Tractatus Logico-Philosophicus* (London: Routledge & Kegan Paul, 1921).

reverse of systematic. This does not mean that it lacked method or rigour. It means rather that there was no part of philosophy which had primacy over any other part. One could start philosophizing at any point, and leave off the treatment of one problem to take up the treatment of another. Philosophy had no foundations, and did not provide foundations for other disciplines. Philosophy was not a house, nor a tree, but a web. This is how we are to understand the famous passage:

> The real discovery is the one that makes me capable of stopping doing philosphy when I want to. – The one that gives philosophy peace, so that it is no longer tormented by questions which bring *itself* into question. Instead, we now demonstrate a method, by examples; and the series of examples can be broken off. Problems are solved (difficulties eliminated) not a *single* problem.[12]

In refusing to countenance systematic or foundationalist metaphysics, Wittgenstein was distancing himself from many of the great philosophers of the past, including Aristotle. For Aristotle there was a philosophical discipline which deserved the title 'First Philosophy'; and the attempt to delineate this is a central theme in the collection of treatises which we know as 'The Metaphysics of Aristotle'. Sometimes first philosophy is described as the discipline which studies being *qua* being; sometimes as the discipline which studies being *qua* divine. The two formulations probably are two ways of describing a single enterprise:

[12] Wittgenstein, *Philosophical Investigations*, 1, 133.

one accounts for everything that is the case about everything there is by appealing ultimately to the divine movers unmoved, and 'the study of being *qua* being' describes this investigation in terms of its explicandum, while 'the study of being *qua* divine' describes it in terms of its explicans. But however one understands Aristotle's first philosophy it is clear that Wittgenstein would have accepted neither its methodological presuppositions nor its foundational role.

However, a considerable part of Aristotle's *Metaphysics* (and of his other works which would nowadays be described as metaphysical) is devoted to a philosophical activity which resembles quite closely Wittgenstein's own method. The distinction between actuality and potentiality, and the classification of different kinds of potentiality, is universally recognized (by both friend and foe) as being one of Aristotle's most characteristic contributions to philosophy, and in particular to the philosophy of mind. His distinctions were later systematized by medieval scholastic philosophers. We might call the systematic study of actuality and potentiality 'dynamic metaphysics'.

Thus, according to Aristotle, active powers (e.g. the power to heat) differed from passive powers (e.g. the power to be heated). Natural powers (such as water's capacity to wet) were to be distinguished from rational powers (such as a pharmacist's ability to prescribe). Natural powers needed certain preconditions for their exercise: fire will only burn wood if the wood is sufficiently dry. But if these conditions are met, then the power will infallibly be exercised. The case is not the same with rational powers. A pharmacist may have the skill to prescribe, and may have the necessary pharmacopea; but he may fail to prescribe if his patient does not have sufficient funds. Natural powers, unlike rational powers, are also *tendencies* to act in a certain manner.

The possession of rational powers, according to Aristotle, is peculiar to human beings. Among the powers of humans there are some which are innate – the senses, for instance – while others, like the ability to play the flute, are acquired by practice. The liberal arts, and in general the skills which are the fruits of education, are powers of a particular kind, namely *dispositions*. Dispositions are *abilities* whose exercises are the relevant scientific, artistic and craft activities; but they are themselves *actualizations* of the capacity to learn which is presupposed by education. They can thus be called actualizations as well as potentialities.

Medieval philosophers introduced a technical terminology here: the skills were first or primary actualizations in contrast to the episodic employment of the skills which were secondary actualizations. Thus the ability to speak Greek is a first actualization, while the actual utterance of a Greek statement or command, or the understanding of a particular Greek text on hearing it, is a secondary actualization.

Wittgenstein undertook a prolonged investigation of the nature of potentiality in *The Brown Book*[13] where

[13] Ludwig Wittgenstein, *The Blue and Brown Books* (Oxford: Blackwell, 1953).

sections 58–67 are devoted to various language-games with the word 'can'. The distinctions which he draws, in writing on the philosophy of mind, between processes and states, and between different kinds of states, correspond to the Aristotelian distinctions between *kinesis*, *hexis* and *energeia*, and the criteria by which the distinctions are made often coincide. The example which Wittgenstein discusses at length to illustrate the relationship between a power and its exercise, namely learning to read,[14] is the same as the standard Aristotelian example of a mental *hexis*, namely, knowledge of grammar.

In addition to the Aristotelian distinction between powers, their possessors and their exercises, we may introduce the notion of the *vehicle* of a power or ability. The vehicle of an ability is the physical ingredient or structure in virtue of which the possessor of an ability possesses the ability and is able to exercise it. The distinction between abilities and their vehicles is not something which is peculiar to human beings and their abilities. Vodka has the power to intoxicate: the vehicle of the power of vodka to intoxicate is the alcohol the vodka contains. A vehicle is something concrete, something which can be weighed and measured. An ability, on the other hand, has neither length nor breadth nor location. This does not mean that an ability is something ghostly: my front-door key's ability to open my front door is not a concrete object, but it is not a spirit either.

[14] Wittgenstein, *Philosophical Investigations*, Vol. 1, pp. 156ff.

An important instance of the distinction between possessor, ability and vehicle is the distinction between people, their minds and their brains. Human beings are living bodies of a certain kind, with various abilities. The mind, as we have said, is the capacity to acquire or possess intellectual abilities. The vehicle of the human mind is, very likely, the human brain. Human beings and their brains are physical objects; their minds are not, because they are capacities. Once again, to say that the mind is not a physical object is not to say that it is a ghostly spirit: denying that the mind has a length or breadth or location does not involve one in spiritualist metaphysics.

In every age since Aristotle, philosophers have been tempted to blur the distinctions he made. In philosophy there is a perennial temptation to reduce potentialities to actualities. Some philosophers attempt to reduce powers to their exercises: thus, explicitly, David Hume, who said the distinction between a power and its exercise was frivolous. Some philosophers attempt to reduce powers to their vehicles: thus, implicitly, Descartes, who wanted to identify the powers of bodies with their geometrical properties.

Philosophical errors about capacities in general show up particularly vividly when they occur in the philosophy of mind. Applied in this area, exercise-reductionism becomes behaviourism: the attempt to identify mind with behaviour consists in treating the complex second-order capacity which is the mind as if it were identical with its particular exercises in behaviour. Applied in this area, vehicle-reductionism becomes materialism: the attempt to identify mind with brain consists in reducing my mental capacities to the parts and structures of my body in virtue of which I possess those capacities.

Materialism is a grosser philosophical error than behaviourism because the connection between a capacity and its exercise is in truth a more intimate one than the connection between a capacity and its vehicle. In the case of the mind, the connection between capacity and exercise is a conceptual connection: one could not understand what the mind was if one did not understand what kinds of thing constitute the exercise of mental capacity. The connection between capacity and vehicle, on the other hand, is a contingent one, discoverable by empirical science. Aristotle's grasp of the nature of mind will stand comparison with that of any subsequent philosopher; but he had a wildly erroneous idea of the relationship of the mind with the brain, which he believed to be an instrument to cool the blood.

Wittgenstein rejected both behaviourism and materialism: in the area of philosophy of mind he is closer to Aristotle and his scholastic successors than he is to any of the more fashionable philosophies of our scientific and scientistic age. In one of his most characteristic and most striking remarks he goes so far as to entertain the possibility that some of our mental capacities may lack a vehicle altogether.

No supposition seems to me more natural than that there is no process in the brain correlated with associating or with thinking; so that it would be impossible to read off thought-processes from brain processes. I mean this: if I talk or write there is, I assume, a system of impulses going out from my brain and correlated with my spoken or written thoughts. But why should the *system* continue further in the direction of the centre? . . . It is thus perfectly possible that certain psychological phenomena *cannot* be investigated physiologically, because nothing corresponds to them . . . Why should there not be a psychological regularity to which *no* physiological regularity corresponds? If this upsets our concept of causality then it is high time it was upset.[15]

Here we see Wittgenstein both at his most anti-metaphysical and at his most metaphysical. He is anti-metaphysical in the sense that he is making a frontal attack on the scientism characteristic of our age: the assumption that there *must* be physical counterparts of mental phenomena. Yet he is here also highly metaphysical. He is not embracing spiritualistic metaphysics: what does the associating, thinking and remembering is a human being with a body, not a spiritual substance. But in the sense of dynamic metaphysics, Wittgenstein is here very close to Aristotle. For he is envisaging as a possibility a pure Aristotelian soul, or entelechy, which operates with no material vehicle: a formal and final cause to which no mechanistic efficient cause corresponds.

We can sum up Wittgenstein's attitude thus: he

[15] Ludwig Wittgenstein, *Zettel* (Oxford: Blackwell, 1967), 608–10.

was hostile to spiritualistic metaphysics and to foundationalist metaphysics; but he was one of the most consummate practitioners of the dynamic metaphysics which is one strand of the Aristotelian tradition. This can be brought out, finally, by pointing to one of the passages in which Wittgenstein most explicitly rejects spiritualistic metaphysics. In this very passage we find that, in the Aristotelian sense, he gives a surprisingly metaphysical formulation of the relationship between soul and body: 'Only of what behaves like a human being can one say that it *has* pains. For one has to say it of a body, or if you like, of a soul which some body *has*. And how can a body *have* a soul.'[16] How striking, that a body's having a soul should seem more problematic than a soul's having a body!

---

[16] Wittgenstein, *Philosophical Investigations*, 1, 283.

12

Wittgenstein on Life, Death and Religion

In recent years, readers have been more interested in the biography of Wittgenstein than in the substance of his philosophy. In this final essay I will try to relate the story of his life to the concerns which have occupied the previous essays.

Ludwig Wittgenstein had as his great-grandfather a land-agent named Moses Maier, who in 1808 took the name of his princely employers, the Wittgensteins. Ludwig's father, Karl, a friend of Johannes Brahms, was the most acute industrialist in the Austrian steel industry: he made the family the Austrian equivalent of the Carnegies or Rothschilds. He had five sons and three daughters by a Catholic wife, and baptized all of them into the Catholic faith. He set out to educate the sons in a very severe regime which would turn them into captains of industry. He did not succeed: three of the sons committed suicide; the fourth, Paul, became (despite the loss of an arm in the Great War) a concert pianist; the fifth, the youngest child, was the philosopher.

Wittgenstein the philosopher attended the *Realschule* in Linz, where he was a contemporary of Adolf Hitler. He was a poor scholar, teased by his peers. At school he lost his faith. The major intellectual influences on him in his youth, apart from the philosophical works of Schopenhauer, were the physicist Boltzmann (suicide 1906) and the psychologist Otto Weininger (suicide 1903).

Wittgenstein's biographer, Raymond Monk,[1] believes that Weininger's bizarre book *Sex and Character*[2] was of fundamental importance in shaping Ludwig's career. According to Weininger – a Jewish homosexual – all human beings are bisexual, a mixture of male and female. Woman is nothing but sexuality: every woman is a mixture of prostitute and mother. Men must choose between the masculine and feminine elements within themselves: the ideal for a man is to free himself from sex. 'The choice that Weininger's theory offers is a bleak and terrible one indeed: genius or death', says Monk, 'if one cannot free oneself from sensuality and earthly desires then one has no right to live at all.'[3]

For Wittgenstein, according to Monk, to acquire genius became a categorical imperative. He once

---

[1] Raymond Monk, *Ludwig Wittgenstein* (New York and Oxford: Macmillan, 1990).

[2] Otto Weininger, *Sex and Character* (Vienna: Fackel, 1903).

[3] Monk, *Wittgenstein*, p. 45.

described Beethoven greeting a friend on completion of a new fugue: he 'came to the door, looking as if he had been fighting the devil, and having eaten nothing for 36 hours because his cook and parlour-maid had been away from his rage'. 'That's the sort of man to be', said Wittgenstein.[4]

It was in Cambridge in 1911 that Wittgenstein first gave evidence of genius in philosophy, and it was Bertrand Russell who first recognized it. Wittgenstein was, he wrote, 'perhaps the most perfect example I have ever known of genius as traditionally conceived, passionate, profound, intense and dominating'.[5] Russell was already well known as the author of powerful, original work in logic and mathematics: he soon realized that Wittgenstein's gifts were greater than his own, and he devoted himself with great generosity to their development. In 1912 he told Wittgenstein's sister, 'We expect the next big step in philosophy to be taken by your brother.'

Wittgenstein as a young man fell in love with philosophy. There was nothing more wonderful in the world, he thought, than the problems of true philosophy. While studying with Bertrand Russell in Cambridge he was gripped and absorbed by philosophical reflection. But he thought of philosophy essentially as a craft. It was an exciting, indeed an obsessive craft, but it was a craft which in its relation to life was no different from music or aeronautics.

[4] Ibid., p. 46.
[5] Bertrand Russell, ibid., p. 55.

Thus he objected to Russell's claim, in his book *Problems of Philosophy*,[6] that philosophy has value. Wittgenstein, as Russell told Lady Ottoline Morrell: 'says people who like philosophy will pursue it and others won't, and there is an end of it'.

Later in his philosophical career he seems to have been of a different opinion: philosophy should be something of special importance in life. Thus, to Norman Malcolm, who at the beginning of the Second World War had made a rash generalization about national character, he said: 'What is the use of studying philosophy if all that it does for you is to enable you to talk with some plausibility about some abstruse questions of logic, etc., and if it does not improve your thinking about the important questions of everyday life?'

The purpose of this essay is to examine Wittgenstein's view of the relationship between philosophy and life. Did he, at least during the greater part of his philosophical career, have a coherent vision here?

There are three separate questions to be answered.

1. What, in Wittgenstein's philosophy, is the role of the concept of life within philosophy itself?
2. What, according to Wittgenstein, is the role of philosophy in ordinary life?
3. Does philosophy – as some philosophers have thought – teach us the meaning of life?

[6] Bertrand Russell, *Problems of Philosophy* (London: Oxford University Press, 1912).

In this essay I will try to answer these three questions from Wittgenstein's writings. But in fairness to Wittgenstein I should explain that I will be drawing mainly on material he never published or intended to publish – letters, diary entries and the like. It may be thought that it is foolish to try to build up a coherent picture from these fragments drawn from different periods of his life. None the less, I think it is possible to do so, with some qualification.

Russell's expectation of Wittgenstein's talent was fulfilled, but the philosophical message was not given to the world until after the Great War. During that war Wittgenstein served in the Austrian army on the eastern and Italian fronts, and much of the material which later appeared in his masterpiece *Tractatus Logico-Philosophicus*[7] was written while on active service. At the front Wittgenstein showed conspicuous courage and was commended and decorated; he was also converted, by the reading of Tolstoy, to an intense though idiosyncratic Christianity. 'Perhaps the near-ness of death', he wrote in his diary, 'will bring me the light of life. May God enlighten me. I am a worm, but through God I become a man. God be with me. Amen.'[8]

In the early notes for the *Tractatus* Wittgenstein claims that the world and life are one. This claim only

[7] Ludwig Wittgenstein, *Tractatus Logico-Philosophicus* (London: Routledge & Kegan Paul, 1921).

[8] Ludwig Wittgenstein, *Notebooks: 1914–16* (Oxford: Blackwell, 1979).

makes sense against a background of solipsism. He has just said that 'The world is my life.' So this dictum means: my world is my life. As Wittgenstein's philosophy developed, he grew out of solipsism. Not that he had ever thought that solipsism was a true doctrine: it was not something that could be said, but something which showed itself. But gradually he came to think that even as a piece of unsayable philosophy solipsism was a perversion of reality.

After the war, having inherited a share of his father's fortune, he found himself one of the wealthiest men in Europe. Within a month of returning he gave all his money away. For some years he supported himself as a gardener or as a schoolmaster in rural schools. He had not ceased to think of philosophy as unimportant: he believed, for a while, that he had already solved all the problems of philosophy in his *Tractatus*, which appeared (after great difficulty in finding a publisher) in German in 1921 and in English in 1922. The book quickly became famous: though it was itself metaphysical and almost mystical, as well as austerely logical, it was most admired by the anti-metaphysical positivists of the Vienna Circle.

It was at Vienna that Wittgenstein returned to the study of philosophy, when his career as a schoolmaster came to an unhappy end after allegations of cruelty to his pupils. Eventually he returned to Cambridge and during his years there in the 1930s he became the most influential teacher of philosophy in Britain. The philosophy which he taught in this period differed from that published in the *Tractatus*; it was not presented in print until *Philosophical Investigations*[9] was published posthumously in 1953.

It was a continuous theme, from Wittgenstein's earliest to his latest writings, that life was not something which came within the purview of natural science. It remained at the boundary of science. But what 'life' means undergoes a change as his own life and philosophy proceeds. In the earlier philosophy it is the solipsistic life of the individual. In the more mature philosophy it is the life of the human community. The inner life has been replaced by the outer life. The life of privacy is replaced by the life of society.

This comes out in the notion, so ubiquitous in Wittgenstein's later philosophy, of language-games. A language-game is intimately connected, for Wittgenstein, with a form of life. The purpose, indeed, of using the expression 'language-game' is to bring out that the speaking of a language is a part of an activity or a form of life. To imagine a language, Wittgenstein says, is to imagine a form of life. To accept the rules of a language is to agree with others in a form of life. The ultimate given in philosophy is not some basis of private experience: it is the forms of life within which we pursue our activities and thought.

What is a form of life? I believe that this concept has often been misunderstood by commentators on Wittgenstein.

There is much talk nowadays of a 'way of life'. A

[9] Ludwig Wittgenstein, *Philosophical Investigations* (Oxford: Blackwell, 1953).

way of life is the kind of thing that used to be invoked to distinguish East and West. The differences between capitalism and communism, we were told, were differences in ways of life. We would not be justified in using nuclear weapons for any small item of policy, we used to be told, but we would be justified in using them to defend our way of life, i.e. to prevent us being taken over by communists. Fortunately, this is now a form of reasoning which has receded into the past. At all events, it is not what Wittgenstein means by 'form of life'.

A way of life may mean, not a difference between two social systems, but a difference between two kinds of career. A monk, for example, has a different way of life from that of a merchant banker. This kind of thing, too, is not what Wittgenstein means by 'form of life'.

Besides 'ways of life' we hear much about lifestyles. Bohemianism is an alternative lifestyle to bourgeois existence; homosexuality is offered as an alternative lifestyle to the life of a family man or woman. This too is utterly different from what Wittgenstein meant by 'form of life'.

The paradigm of a difference between forms of life is the difference between the life of two different species of animals – animals with different 'natural histories', to use an expression beloved by Wittgenstein. Lions have a different form of life from humans; that is why, if a lion could speak, we could not understand him.

But there can be differences between forms of life between human beings too, as G.H. von Wright has made clear from Wittgenstein's late work *On*

Certainty.[10] There the notion of form of life is connected with the notion of '*Weltbild*' or 'world-picture'. Thus Wittgenstein wrote: 'My life shows that I know or am certain that there is a chair over there, or a door, and so on . . . I would like to regard this certainty, not as something akin to hastiness or superficiality, but as a form of life.'[11]

A world-picture is neither true nor false. Disputes about truth are possible only within a world-picture between disputants who share the same form of life. When one person denies what is part of the world-picture of another this may sometimes seem like lunacy, but sometimes a very deep difference of culture. If someone doubts that the world has existed before he was born we might think him mad: but in a certain culture might not a king be brought up in the belief that the world began with him?

So much for the role played by life in Wittgenstein's philosophy. Forms of life are the data which philosophy cannot call into question but which are presupposed by any philosophical enquiry. Let us turn to the other side of the relationship: if forms of life have to be accepted as given, how can philosophy have any effect on the living of our daily life?

Well, what is the function of philosophy? Wittgenstein said it was to untie the knots in our thinking. To do that it must make complicated movements; but the results of philosophy are as simple as a plain piece of

[10] Ludwig Wittgenstein, *On Certainty* (Oxford: Blackwell, 1969).
[11] Ibid., Section 166.

string. The complexity of philosophy derives not from any specially complex subject-matter but from the entanglement of our knotted understanding.

Sometimes Wittgenstein depicts philosophy as a therapy; at other times it is portrayed as something which gives an overall understanding of our language, and hence of our world.

Philosophy for Wittgenstein is a therapy: it cures the bruises we get by banging our understanding against the limits of language. The philosopher is like a psychoanalyst who encourages us to express doubts and puzzlement which we have been taught to repress; he cures us of the nonsense we nurture in our minds by encouraging us to bring it out to the light of day, turning latent nonsense into patent nonsense. Philosophy's role, so defined, seems negative: it seems to be of use only to those whose intellect is sick.

But Wittgenstein also speaks of philosophy as giving a special kind of understanding. It gives us a clear view of the way in which we use words, and thus of the world which we grasp by means of the concepts of our language. The function of philosophy is to establish order in our knowledge of the use of language – to discover, if you like, the essence of language, not by looking for some hidden metaphysical machinery within it, but by bringing into clear view what we all of us already confusedly know.

Philosophy does not discover any new truths. Philosophical problems are solved not by giving new information but by arranging what we have always known in a way which prevents us overlooking what is in itself most obvious. The right kind of philosophy, by removing the problems generated by false philosophy, allows us to have a clear view of what we are doing when we are using language non-philosophically in our ordinary life.

But if the value of philosophy is simply that it gets rid of philosophical worries, why do philosophy at all – would it not be simpler never to look at a book of philosophy? Philosophy, Wittgenstein thought, is nothing over and above philosophical problems. But if you never get as far as the problems, you will never need the solutions. Why do philosophy if it is only useful against philosophers?

Wittgenstein's answer is this: Philosophy is only useful against philosophers, but within each one of us, whether we know it or not, there is already a philosopher. There is a philosophy embedded in the very language we use. This philosophy is not a set of theories or propositions: it is embodied in the misleading nature of the surface grammar of natural languages, which disguises the actual way in which words are used, the real or deep grammar.

Language exercises a tyranny, a bewitchment over us. We can only extricate ourselves from this by rebelling against language, fighting the urgent temptation to misrepresent to ourselves the way in which we really use words. Philosophy demands an effort not so much of the intellect as of the will. The sacrifice which philosophy demands is in itself no great one: the renunciation of certain combinations of words as senseless. Yet it can be a cruelly difficult abnegation.

Philosophical misunderstanding will not harm us if we restrict ourselves to everyday tasks, using words within the language-games which are their primitive homes. But if we start upon abstract studies – of mathematics, say, or of psychology, or of theology – then our thinking will be hampered and distorted unless we can free ourselves of philosophical confusion. Intellectual enquiry will be corrupted by mythical notions of the nature of numbers or of the mind or of the soul.

Philosophical therapy, then, is essential if one is to make a success of any but the simplest tasks of life. (For many people, the conclusion to be drawn is not that they should take up philosophy but that they should adopt a very simple form of life.) But it does not follow from this that philosophy is any sort of guide to life. The physician, after all, when he has healed his patient does not tell his patient what to do with his healthy life. Has the philosopher any more right to tell others how to live? Can philosophy, as some philosophers have thought, teach us the meaning of life?

Throughout his life Wittgenstein denied that either science or philosophy could express the meaning of life. In the *Tractatus* he wrote: 'We feel that even when all possible scientific questions have been answered, the problems of life remain completely untouched. Of course, there are then no questions left, and this itself is the answer.'[12]

---

[12] Wittgenstein, *Tractatus*, 6.52.

What are the problems of life? Two questions may come to mind. First, what shall I do with my life? Second, what is the meaning of life? Some people might question whether these two questions are distinct. If the only meaning to my life is a meaning I myself give to it then the two questions are the same; but that is not something which can be taken for granted. Some philosophers – some existentialists, for instance – have thought that a prerequisite for facing up to the first question was a realization that there was no answer to the second.

Wittgenstein's position was different. It is true that he thought that the solution of the problem of life was to be found in the vanishing of the problem. But this did not mean that life was necessarily meaningless. What it meant was that nothing that one could say, whether as scientist or as philosopher, could *state* the meaning of life. If life has a meaning, it is something which cannot be said but which must show itself.

But what would be a meaningful life? We get some idea of what a meaning*less* life is from an oft-quoted letter which Wittgenstein wrote to his friend Engelmann.

> I had a task, did not do it, and now the failure is wrecking my life. I ought to have done something positive with my life, to have become a star in the sky. Instead of which I remained stuck in the earth, and now I am gradually fading out. My life has really become meaningless, and so it consists only of futile episodes.[13]

[13] In Paul Engelmann (ed.), *Letters from Ludwig Wittgenstein, with a Memoir* (Oxford: Blackwell, 1967), p. 41.

To see the meaning of life would be to have a conviction that life was worth living. By contrast with a meaningless succession of disconnected episodes, a meaningful life would be one which constituted the fulfilment of a task. But if there is a task, who sets the task? Some would say that it is for each person to set their own task in life. That is not Wittgenstein's answer. For him, the setter of the task is God. But to say that is not so much to answer the question as to give a definition of 'God'. 'To believe in God', he wrote in a First World War notebook, 'means to see that life has a meaning.'

God is the setter of the task and the judge of its performance. When Wittgenstein discussed religion in his classes, the central role was often played by the concept of judgement. Thus:

Suppose somebody made this guidance for this life: believing in the Last Judgement. Whenever he does anything, this is before his mind . . . This in one sense must be called the firmest of all beliefs, because the man risks things on account of it which he would not do on things which are by far better established for him.[14]

What gives life meaning, we might say, is faith. But how does Wittgenstein conceive of faith? He is most unsympathetic to the view that faith consists in assent to a doctrine:

[14] Ludwig Wittgenstein, *Lectures on Religious Belief* (Oxford: Blackwell, 1966), p. 53.

Christianity is not a doctrine, not I mean a theory about what has happened and what will happen to the human soul, but a description of something that actually takes place in human life. For 'consciousness of sin' is a real event and so are despair and salvation through faith.[15]

This might be a plausible contention about writers such as Bunyan (whom Wittgenstein had in mind in writing this passage). It would not be plausible about the gospels. Wittgenstein admits that these have the form of historical narratives. But their role in Christianity, he maintains, is not to provide a historical foundation for Christian belief.

Christianity is not based on a historical truth rather it offers us a (historical) narrative and says: now believe. But not, believe this narrative with the belief appropriate to a historical narrative; rather: believe through thick and thin, which you can do only as a result of a life. Here you have a narrative; don't take the same attitude as you take to other historical narratives. Make quite a different place in your life for it. There is nothing paradoxical in that.[16]

Wittgenstein was most opposed to the idea that Christianity was *reasonable*. He thought that Christians based enormous things upon flimsy evidence; they were obviously not reasonable. This did not mean that they were unreasonable; it meant that they did not treat faith as a matter of reasonability.

[15] Ludwig Wittgenstein, *Culture and Value* (Oxford: Blackwell, 1980), p. 28.
[16] Ibid., p. 32.

Some Christians believe that faith, though not proved by reason, is a reasonable state of mind; some claim that there can be a natural theology which is a branch of philosophy. Wittgenstein, by contrast, makes a sharp contrast between faith and philosophy. Philosophy cannot give meaning to life. At best philosophy could provide wisdom, and Wittgenstein frequently contrasts the emptiness of wisdom with the vigour of faith. Faith is a passion, but wisdom is cold grey ash, covering up the glowing embers.

But though only faith, and not philosophy, can give meaning to life, that does not mean that philosophy has no rights whatever within the terrain of faith. Faith may involve talking nonsense, and philosophy may point out that it is nonsense. Wittgenstein, who once said, 'Whereof one cannot speak, thereof one must be silent', later said, 'Don't be afraid of talking nonsense.' But he went on to add: 'You must keep an eye on your nonsense.'[17]

It is philosophy that keeps an eye on the nonsense. First, it points out that the nonsense *is* nonsense: faith is no more able than philosophy to *say* what is the meaning of life. It does not matter, Wittgenstein thought, if the gospels are false. One could not say that of something which was a *saying*, since the most important fact about sayings is that they are either true or false, and it matters greatly which. Secondly, among the utterances which are not sayings, philosophy still

[17] Ibid., p. 56.

212

has a critical role. Above all, it can distinguish faith from superstition. The attempt to make religion appear reasonable seemed to Wittgenstein to be the extreme of superstition.

If this is Wittgenstein's vision of the meaning of life, has he anything to offer about the meaning of death? Death does indeed have meaning for him, but not by being the gate to an afterlife. Even if one could believe in immortality, it would not confer meaning; nothing is solved by surviving for ever. An eternal life would be as much a riddle as this one.

Wittgenstein, in his later philosophy, makes much of the social context of philosophy. Yet his own life was one of solitude, spiritual and often physical. His genius is patent to any philosopher who will take the time and trouble to come to grips with his profound but difficult writings. His life, as described by Monk, seems to have been a lonely and tragic one. He was often tormented by temptations to suicide, and was sometimes on the verge of mental illness. He regarded his life as a university professor as 'a living death', and held many of his colleagues, in the various callings he pursued, in loathing and contempt. His only philosophical peer was Russell, and the relationship between the two soured after his return to Cambridge. Many of his philosophical disciples loved him, but it was a love mixed strongly with fear.

Faith in God was important to Wittgenstein, but his faith seems to have been a sombre one. God was perhaps no more than Fate. If he was to be thought of as a person, it was solely as a severe judge. If death has meaning, it is precisely as an end, a final end, of life. Wittgenstein described his father's death as beautiful, as a death worth a whole life. Perhaps, indeed, the test of a good life was that it was one that issued in a good death.

Did Wittgenstein's own life match his ideal of the relationship between philosophy and life? His letters and diaries constantly draw attention to the mismatch he felt between aspiration and execution. But if the criterion of a good life is that it leads to a welcome death, we must remember that Wittgenstein's last message to his friends on his deathbed was that his life had been wonderful.

One of the papers in Wittgenstein's *Nachlass* is a poem that he presented to a friend. It is not an easy poem to translate: but I offer the following as an English version of it.

Once true love's scented veil about my head you cast
Then every gesture of your hands,
Each tender movement of your limbs,
Does leave my soul bereft of sense.

Can you catch it when it flutters?
When each tiny gentle movement
Traces deep down in my heart it marks.

When morning makes its bells to ring
The gardener walks through his garden realm
Walking on tiptoe on the earth he owns
And every flower awakes and wondering stares
Up at that shining, tranquil face.
Who was it, then, that wove around your feet

214

That veil whose touch we feel like gossamer?
Is the wind's breeze, too, at your beck and call?
Is it the spider's, or the silkworm's work?

The poem is not easy to interpret, without knowledge of the original circumstances of its composition
and presentation. Clearly, however, the principal theme
is the veil that love casts over the relationship between a
lover and a beloved. The poem ends with the question
whether that veil is an adornment (the work of the
silkworm) or a trap (the work of the spider)?

What kind of love is in question? The key may perhaps be given by the section about the gardener, which
itself is quite puzzling in the context. I conjecture that
the passage may be intended to invite us to recall the
twentieth chapter of the fourth gospel in which Mary
Magdalen encounters the risen Jesus early on the morning of the first day of the week.

> She saw Jesus standing, and knew not that it was Jesus. Jesus
> saith unto her, 'Woman, why weepest thou? Who seekest
> thou?' She, supposing him to be the gardener, said unto
> him, 'Sir, if you have borne him hence, tell me where thou
> hast laid him, and I will take him away.' Jesus saith unto her,
> 'Mary.' She turned herself, and saith unto him, 'Rabboni,'
> which is 'Master'. Jesus saith unto her: 'Touch me not; for I
> am not yet ascended to my Father.'
> (John 20, 14–17)

The references in Wittgenstein's poem to the early
morning, to the church bells, to the gardener with
supernatural powers all fit this association: they call up
an image of many a renaissance *Noli me Tangere* with

215

Jesus holding a gardener's tool and Mary Magdalen kneeling at his feet. If this identification is correct, then the kind of love of which the poet is principally thinking is that of a religious believer for a religious master. The question, then, with which Wittgenstein's poem ends is the question which haunts the life of every person who is genuinely agnostic: is religion a snare and a delusion, or is it something precious and glorious?

Index

INDEX

218